LOADING TERMINAL

Published 2022 by the87press

The 87 Press LTD

87 Stonecot Hill

Sutton

Surrey

SM3 9HJ

www.the87press.co.uk

Loading Terminal © Danny Hayward, 2022

Cover Image: Geistervölker © Ines Doujak, 2021

The moral right of Danny Hayward has been asserted in accordance with the Copyright, Designs and Patents Act 1988

ISBN: 978-1-7399547-6-5

Design: Stanislava Stoilova [www.sdesign.graphics]

Printed and bound by CPI Group (UK) Ltd, Croydon, CR0 4YY

Table of Contents

Climate and Resilience

for mv
'having principles is a privilege not everyone can afford' ...
is more of a background hum

death isn't real yet,

it's a technology of the future, all the roses grown seethrough
and the hot, rainless materialism I need you don't leave me

nor burn like a fever in the idiotic grey light.
the erectile tissue of lips is drifting, hot rainless

illegible funerals granted to the Safdie brothers for having
        destroyed art.
This live event has now ended

pinned feverish smear worlds I don't want this to be clear
fist illegible spilt crude on the runway anyway all it says is
        pig words

'I have cried, I have made decisions and then rejected them,
I have plunged from madness into madness'

inequality in the Phalanstère say lets toast the whole area

* * * * * * * * * *

Splitscreen. Six US Congresspeople climb through barbwire,
thornwire, clawwire and lipwire. Tokyo peeling, various
impressions of a splitscreen. A body on the ground. A note
in its hand reads, 'I accept the reduction of my thinking
to the generally known and accepted. I accept the wasting
of my language to a mere instrument in the permanent
competition for visibility'. Speech sounds, swallowed
up by a hospital's high ceiling. Caribbean receptionist,
Mediterranean security guard. Split

* * * * * * * * * *

In future all immigration vans to move with impossible

slowness through an endless sea of people who hate them

Split

everyone I see in the queue to Breadland is peeling
White British poets, Caribbean receptionists
An art I ruined because I hated it
without understanding
White sleets of wallpaper in the bulletproof vehicle
what balenciaga art skinheads with tiny fragments for
memories, did

you fucking snitch
live.
silent train carriages are rinsing depthless ended

* * * * * * * * * * *

And so the stamen crumbles, its dream wasted along with
all other dreams. cries in the dark trains, orbiting the earth.

Darktown, Website City.
poetry stumbles through my mind in distress,
'aesthetic leftism' written in black paint on the high,
            invisible walls.
People are freaking out, getting off on their veto power over art
other than a lack of love and a lack of understanding and a
            lack of being human and a lack of caring

* * * * * * * * * * *

I don't talk about art in terms of intentions or meaning
Art for me is just a species of distortion
the decideability of some nouns, some verbs,

and the subjects of verbs is more important to me
than life, 'activism', or the development of precise knowledge
When I look up at the sky, at the blood
raining upwards, the ice shells of Europa
collapsing in shows of force, while the snow
falls inside our cells like a distorted species
Of music, everything falls suddenly into place
Israel is destroyed the balcony outside my room is sunk into
        a garden
Never-images reverse from the police culture
in fire across my eyelids mixed with night
and vanish like palindromes I don't use anymore.
Though words like race or class fail suddenly
certain things persist, a reading of poetry
by Galina Rymbu, Florence Uniacke
and Laurel Uziell lasts forever surviving
inside us, opposed to all other experiences
Will bleeds out the eyelids, tone-death, whites
on the dust in our eyeslips'
J-P G balconies and ice rainbows melt
Reality all the latest hip theory fetishes
in the under-nouns crawl like signs of image-death,
music-death, motion-death, Six of them
symbols pockmarking the streets of Balenciaga
ballistic freezing plantations
turn lanterns flower, and vanish like individuals
who are the limit and walled reach of this world:
These States Exist. now Man Passes on
but States remain for Ever he passes thro
them like a traveller who may
as well suppose that the places he has passed thro
exist no more Slogan
art was in me like a bayonet, driven through
Israel all others were outside me, like a symbol

Anna Kavan inside our cells a distorted music echoes
a distorted space falls into shape.
When I look up at the sky, everything falls suddenly into place.
The balcony outside my room is sunk into a garden.
If certain events occur in the mind
Our experiences will last forever
Israel is not a state, states are eternal
When they invent death we will find ways to use it

* * * * * * * * * * *

How is it we have walked through fires and are not
consumed
how is it we have made art able to exist in states without

raising those states to be as the state of Israel is we are not blinded by
that
wish we have walked thru LA trauma existentialism states not one of us

succumbed to image-death each of us passed through
that
heaven never submitted to its authority never found intimacy with it erotic

Let it come to that, in the van debate poverty equals.
Banality that defines us as a link of simple alternatives.
I touch you like an idiot town centre chain store emailed to you shortly
as the music of the escalator gnaws its tumour through Los Angeles

Let it ram blue my image habit waste in the night's peremptory sweetness. I can
see the phone in your voice I just can't see when you're speaking
to banalise depending on the blank crisis word now
I can't even watch the news worms die, in their bellowing hollow oceans.

Wind from other planets, unutterably basic as our hearts are
let them come now, like a smoke breaks out the van's dark scabbed over windows.
New worms we die new, like LA how many ages hence
I don't care what sails through form-death, let the sails curve. We won't row back

CR = May 2021. *Thanks W. Blake, Sophie Carapetian, Paul Celan, Deli Girls, Faiz Ahmad Faiz, Franz Kafka, Anna Kavan, Nathaniel Mackey, Galina Rymbu, Arnold Schoenberg, Algernon Swinburn, Delia Torres, Florence Uniacke, Laurel Uziell.*

I/II

to Michael Kimble,
for the masks 2 survive

Crude Teutons stalk about in the No-Go Area
and spit on a flaming rag doll. Welcome to a sheen of
generative ambiguity
settling over a UV magnetic cauldron under the influence of
a rampant shadow,
welcome to snow falls in horizontal sheets,
seen through a sheen of hope even fucking gasps like one,
welcome love, welcome gentleness,
sheen of puppet gasping for a stick figure.
Outside painted unlit is affected to be fixed.
Welcome stick figure, welcome puppet,
to a leaden scene of generative ambiguity;
reality doesn't have to be anything like this,
sheen of despair helps to forget about that.
Welcome surface effect including snow
and a draft torn open in the leaden streetlight.
Welcome gamut rips through the surface.
Start again.
Sophisticated Teutons stalk about in the Knowledge Quarter
under roasted streetlights and spit on a flaming rag doll.
Once again intuitions swing
from the sketched-in lampposts; once again cartoon
veins ripped from history drain artfully into a pronounced
gutter.
Stick figures get obliterated,
a Headless Chicken tries to feel something.
The end wears the mask of the beginning
it tore off, groping through the insane waves
of reality looking for the cause of
a fire sweeping through the corridor
of sentimental outrage; middle-
class disembodied screams reopening
as a debased coffee shop tearing
its mask off in a cloud of UV fog.

Now watch the shadow
peel off from its former self, announce something
nuanced about mayors, etcetera.
Will we never stagger out from under the shadow
of happiness, sing it in the street,
in the carnival we had to cancel because
the fascists turned up, it happens anyway,
everything happens anyway, all pleasure,
all struggles, through the snow falling in horizontal sheets,
fascist puppets come and go on the fucking internet
but we get out of there, listless unreality
sweetened by a charade of mindlessness
to the uttermost degree of unreality, through
the doors swinging in the cartoon tornado;
moving past election posters torn down then
swept about atmospherically, stick figures thickening
in the Victory Square, getting high on
listless unreality, now sweetened by
a charade, watching the hatchery burn.
Just another ordinary day. Money goes
where it fucking well wants.
Now welcome to the real beginning,
when the Shadow resolves into
a Shadow of its Former Self
and there are two Mayors you need to find:
one to kill and the other who will
solve everything. How's that for a plot point. Two mayors
you need to find: one who will solve everything and the other
to kill. You are the Shadow who is a Shadow of its Former Self,
the skies burn in lush colours,
troops file past in formation,
applause rises from the assembled
masses of wounded pigs, each more
beautiful and more complex than the last, each dreaming of

a National Culture more febrile and immense than the last,
a change of seismic truth and reality,
half-listening to the warm-up speaker,
as you push past them, into the lesser exactitude of need,
near to Casablanca's Caribbean Cuisine, and the other
market houses,
and the other street corners, each more grey and imprecise
than the last,
each more general and symbolic than the last, past the
drunks frozen
to death and the neighbours you barely speak to, each more
the essence of a ferocious contraction in reality than the last,
past the imprecise nights, the elliptical, casual days;
past displacement, past sincerity,
the stick figures now doubled over on the stairs
to The Non-Vacuum,
cartoons doing kitchen work in the high street bars,
past white triangles hassling small shopkeepers,
past teenagers dragged into a vacant rectangle,
past the synthetic upheaval of a merely technical urgency,
through flakes
of rain, languishing in the soft light of a
café redeployed as a single, hovering
point, past the synthetic urgency
of a merely technical upheaval, through sheets
of rain, each more crudely rendered than the last,
through the crowds of
card sharps and delivery people,
through youth,
an enigmatic glow, and the c19 blizzard that envelops it,
through urban life, its arid, ungrammatical corridors,
its portals of raw violence, its stunted, out-of-focus ecstasy
broken down and reassembled in the kiosk
next to U & I Trimmings, its maimed tone,

through all of this, this single, clean, inert surface,
crowds of personifications screaming or dying
in lush colours, headless chickens wearing
sandwich boards outside the third tier of cultural rapture,
luxury bedsits, early weekday evenings
of aggressive mimicry, the official opening of the Retraction
of Intimacy
in the Square of the People, jumbled, kinetic, dazzling and loud,
the Beheaded Phantasms selling
CDs near the front entrance,
the cold hills at the back, kids on benches,
a cut and paste Ecstasy rising through mounting frost
from its car door towards the savage renewal of meaningless
consensus;
past energy, past listlessness, past Low Cost Tropical Food,
past the burned out shell of Feeling I and the
refurbished facade of Feeling II,
past the cut-and-paste memory who cries out to
Ecstasy sweeping into the Retraction of Intimacy that it used
to be called A Joy Re-Risen From The Depths of Non-
Violence,
and the private party of shiftless unreality
dominated by the full simulator of collective agency
and its inflamed
screen of depopulated ironies,
set up in the bar on the top floor of Sadism, from which
Dream and Understanding look out
over a contrived ache,
premonition of a new gutter
opening next door to a new drain
and past kfh.co.uk;
past night and day,
and Abermale and Dabakh,
the alcoholics

in the churchyard
listening to music of an intricate and sustaining
indifference,
the stagnant detail of schools and council workers
dragged into the aroused underside of a grey clamp locked
in struggle
with itself,
as if it were as easy
to change life into a music of hurtful and excessive plainness
as it is to
drill a hole in a dull square
and to watch
as reality ebbs from it;
past anguish,
past incantation,
the collapsed dancehall and its sacrificed interior,
the outlines moved on in the interest of tonal integrity,
the cops standing around with the smokers
outside the betting shop
in the political subtext, just waiting
for something to fucking happen,
in an atmosphere of lush and expansive violence;
and past the Beheaded Phantasm whose slogan is I have no
time for you,
pushing through the crowd of pigs
in the wavering, unsteady light of
an ostentatious winter,
at the dead-
centre of the rigged square and its
fenced-off area, beyond the
medic pumping at the chest of a bleeding effigy
in the half-light near the boarded-
up concentration
camp, staring up

at the swirl of colour on the mega-
screen
with a painful and unwarrantable nakedness, as if
to reassure itself
of whatever meaning it read there,
insensible to the
parade of torchbearers
and the kids turning over a car
near to the nameless
drugstore;
past the Beheaded Phantasm whose slogan is I have no time
for you,
the lip of compassion trembling in the exposed stairwell of
defeat, looking out beyond the
mechanical floats to the faint outline of experience
rising up in a haze of cremated sweat,
the vein torn out of 2011 and set like a jewel in the
mutilated arm of 2016,
throwing its shadow
over the broken figurines
selling brittle concrete masks outside the
shuttered restaurants and the
literal art galleries,
in the carnival of dilapidated intuition, under an abused sky
twinkling with antipathy
and past the ex-repair centre re-opened as a fear of melting
and the erased sweat backing up in a similar incident
strenuously denied by
a smear of ash,
past the Indian restaurants in the Bengali area;
and past the sheets of passive mist
rolling over the pawn shops and antique dealers,
each thinner and more figurative than the last,
each more like a crayon

stick figure pissing blood
in a back alley of euphoric indirection
than the last; the dotted outlines just trying to get warm,
the nameless service depots and small businesses,
the teenagers in the basketball court,
a life of mere invective just trying to get warm,
two parallel lines conducting a discrete exchange in a livid
simulation of night;
past all this, the windows already shut up,
the street aswarm with vipers,
the presently meaningless crowd disturbance
spilling carelessly into a new decade
amid the red-hot atmosphere of
over-conceptualised speechlessness, wind tearing through
the gaps in reality, despair rising in the vanguard parade
of caved-in vultures,
the Headless Chicken Who Wears a Mask 2 Survive slipping
away, gently
into the forecourt of contained grief, the raw clamour of
clowns staggering
outside the complex bed and breakfast beneath the dull strobe
of the same streets and the same skies, slipping in and out of
consciousness
like the ravaged world in a small room at the back of nothing,
amid the first, isolated howls of despair,
amid enigmatic bullshit, the exaggerated slow motion of
declared empathy,
the frozen block of our own prohibited nakedness, the stick
figures crowding into
a small room at the back of nothing, the tedious alternation of
theory and practice in the strophic vertigo of today
vanishing on repeat
with enigmatic clarity, the thick odour of
why bother hanging over the rubber-proofing works and

spreading into the hiatus
between metaphor and concept,
sold off to an unidentified assailant
wearing a The Mayor mask over its burnt grate,
invisible to the streams of white triangles with drawn faces,
the troops standing around outside the billiard hall,
past caring about whether something fucking happens or not,
looking on as a puppet is thrown out
of The Non-Vacuum and swept
along the main thoroughfare by a great
concourse of humanity, caved-in vultures at their head,
bearing on their shoulders the body of Mayor I,
eyes bursting from their sockets like two exploding boilers
you need to find, one to kill and the other who will solve
everything;
we go past all that,
past the faded signs of last week's socialism,
the howls mingling with
the choir of parishioners trans-
fixed by their watercolour stab wounds,
amid the conflicting surfaces in the depths of the world,
abstract and beautiful like planes
of ice kicked in at the front of Feeling II, pigs swarming into it,
setting fire to its hated plenitude;
we go past all of that,
past where the formal stasis of violent excess dissolves into
a dog eating a dog in a side alley,
troubled by the economic aspirations of raw feeling
going through the motions,
or staring up dreamily through a glass ceiling at the ravaged
basis of
a dynamic world,
or pacing up and down the railway siding of an obsolete
and predetermined escalation,

looking out over plain common sense with its eyes swollen shut
next to the immigration advice centre with its files
strewn everywhere,
we go
past all
that;
past the excessive violence of formal stasis,
the facial composites for the Beheaded Phantasm
whose slogan is I have no time for you pasted up everywhere,
across the huge gasometers and in the rotten shells of the
real estate brokers,
past the bridge of endurance,
from which a puppet plunges into speech and is
duly sucked beneath it;
past days going by unsteadily,
the downsize risk of an abstract restlessness
becoming derelict among the corpses
scattered around in the inert goods corridor;
through nightclubs in which bombs go on and off wordlessly.
I think that in the ease of imagining cruelty on any scale
and in the therapeutic restitution
of the self to which that imagined cruelty leads
I can begin to understand how much more beautiful it is to
want to smash my own head in.
From damage reflected into its own origin, the struggle to
love others
radiates as it might from the torn up roots of an instinct
once opposed to fascism.
The Headless Chicken knows it. The Beheaded Phantasm
fucking knows it.
Anyone living in the shadow of a non-progressive drive
redeveloped
as a retail complex of historical imposition
knows it;

even Mr. Interior Minister and the Disembowelled Grid
wearing a Mask Because It Fucking Can,
even they *suspect* it,
standing around
outside the ambiguous motorcycle club,
watching as you go by, throwing your shadow
that is the shadow of a shadow who is the shadow of its
former self
across the unenduring day care centre,
the churches and mosques, the fluorescent self-criticism
flashing at eye level the street price of revulsion,
as you push past the crowds of middlemen,
the right-wing sports bars, the meaningless dull light,
the blinking collage of de-eroticised services through which
a legless antagonism wheels itself
past Feeling I,
offset by rain erupting into a surface effect
in the concave openness of
decanted estates and grey squares;
past the primary schools and furniture stores
and throughout the beige locking mechanism of estate
agents and construction sites:
blisters rising from the unchangeable hierarchy of any surface,
its fucking roots spreading
over the vegetable markets and clawing at the corner stores
and thickening in the political and moral atmosphere
of a net closing;
you go past all that,
the screwed up crayon face
dragging me through the park gates on its spindle legs,
the lustreless cavities shrugging and
climbing in and out of taxis, coming and going in the
members' clubs,
asking about the editorials in *Pimp Convulsion* on the evil

decrees of the refugee government,
the signs proving cruelty is a gateway
to a reality made inexpugnable by delusion,
pale stick figures watching as unhappiness bent over by a
lamppost coughs up an itch
and is bought up by it,
the free market in which pleasure flourishes for a second
and is then
torn down in 1934 to make way for a fascist brothel
franchised to Feeling II under the name A Quality More
Complex and More Open than Irony,
Darker and More Exultant than Hope with a gift store
called The Real Enemy;
and past the hateful crests of remorse, the atmospheric
extremism of checks and balances
fogging up the windows of the derelict community centre,
now re-opening as a faithful, nostalgic reconstruction of
Feeling I,
that Some Stick Figures really are Taking the Piss,
bathed in UV or numb with Feeling II,
or tearing at their masks,
in these streets,
among these houses, amid these plumes of smoke,
wondering how much of their face will come
off, choking,
pushing past the soap box from which the Headless Chicken
who wears a Mask 2 Survive
screams of
the spine of history,
which speaks to you
in the language of electric shocks
or not at all,
into the local community, where non-political wishes
rot candidly into fantasies of self-harm,

amid vultures, blossoming in simulated carnage
and the smokers still standing around outside the pool hall
after all these years,
watching as you go by, throwing your shadow
that is the shadow of a shadow who is the shadow of its
former self
across the street where Dream and Understanding hand out
flyers for a demo
in support of the Beheaded Phantasm whose slogan is I have
no time for you,
vigilante pigs pushing past the stewards arriving in advance
of the cavalcade of Mayor II,
the one who will solve or kill everything,
boiler steam rising in UV plumes,
falling in grey slants across stray pages of *Pimp Convulsion*
twisting
in the misanthropic crux of perceived life, soup kitchens,
road blocks, masks trodden underfoot outside a decayed
terminal,
the sprung car boot of the lower stage of socialism
crashed into the collapsed stage set of Feeling II
and an unnatural ideology still trussed up by anaesthesia
climbing from it;
past all of this, in search either of a total worldview
or the direct expression of the shadow that daily obliterates it,
never deciding between the two
but stumbling along the receding fissure of the convulsion
towards its checkpoint
and treating that blockage as if it were itself erotogenic,
wanting to be as clear as possible,
looking at and loving the ordinary world
with two dots for eyes,
wanting only to hate the right things,
only to come out with yet more

abstract talk
like that,
yet more Mayor II talk,
yet another reality eating competition
talk, twice as fast again every year talk, of legal action
against the owners of Feeling Eins
talk of an upturn of talk talk
of the town talk over three floors in a flagship extremity talk,
of free masks with every gulped back
ragged fucking protest talk,
love talk, fucking love talk,
got to love it talk of sorry
can't stop talk of
a fascist brothel replicated on a pinhead
who talks on the Mega Screen through a crayon line mouth
of a merger ruled out by talk
of a downturn at Feeling II in talks to divest its struggling
gift shop, what was it called,
real talk, constructive talks, talk of Feeling III
around the corner each year twice as fast
talk ripped out with Take-Ur-Job
on a Feeling I bender, looking up at
Feeling II with talk of a human face scrawled on
twice as fast, was it the Real Enemy,
watching unconfessed Feelings going by
on the truncated pavement of raw sensation,
with no respite, and no muting the phasing sirens
of stagnation and dynamism
in the analogical sector of the cartoon economy
with its live action humans and its two departments
of viscera and masks,
blinking amid the UV flares and rootless seizures
of a Non-Vacuum non-profit, no joke,
no exit from the cartoon economy

but a stick up in our own gift shop;
the Beheaded Phantasm knows it, the Headless Chicken
fucking knows it,
the shadow of a shadow who is the shadow of its former self
thickens with the knowledge of it,
pushing through the crowd towards the Mega Screen
where Mayor III appears,
watching unconfessed Feelings going by
on the truncated pavement of raw sensation, who look on
into the crowd of thuggish cones
dragging a sphere from a
white plane, chanting about how the underbelly of ecstasy
is musical, wearing Feeling I Wears a Feeling II Mask 2 Survive
t-shirts covered in erased blood stains
in a gutter too deeply wrenched out
from a comic haze of UV shadows
as in abstract art, class violence and national sentimentalism
in that order, amid these streets
and these chimneys sliding from these crayon houses,
and these crude Teutons making a getaway
in a squeal of squiggle wheels past the closed GPs
and the specialist clinic for people who want their nerve endings
to look like stricken pendulums, doing a roaring business,
this the shadow knows,
this you know, beyond a shadow of a doubt,
past street lights shining on the crust of a damaged idiom,
the universal deluge as a grey smear,
a stick figure drawing itself with no arms,
with a sign saying We make ourselves,
in every sports bar in the irreducible metropolitan
gyroscope, caked with night and panic
and decomposing beneath the floorboards of
a merely technical urgency,
we make ourselves, staggering

into the day with our repertoire of schemes
past squares shooting up squiggles
beneath the UV signs that scream No Win No Feeling II,
we make ourselves,
and above it the city is obliterated,
spat on by the manikin with the snake gut
carrying a briefcase
with the arm that sprouts from his head
we make ourselves;
past the stick figure menaced by cylinders
barely out of their teens,
past cop cars like fingerprints in a mirror;
past a small and recognisable world,
idiotically cramped into the top corner of an endless clearing,
past Fucking Hell Man saying fucking hell man to
the shadow of the shadow who is a shadow
of its former self, moving past the assembled
masses of wounded pigs observing on the Mega Screen
Mayor III hold aloft the head of the Beheaded Phantasm
whose slogan is I have no time for you,
amid the first, isolated howls of bloodlust,
in spite of a class analysis with a charge of 1 or 0,
later injected into the roof of the mouth of 2011;
and past the torn down wall newspaper,
the scraps of its analysis of
progressive liberalism twisting
prettily in the air, images of the phantom head
of the beheaded phantasm
rolling its crayon eyes,
past ritual bullshit, past cleansing bullshit,
towards the dark stage
where destiny awaits, too much to bear 4 one
mask slipping 2 survive
and too much 4 one mind 2 Feel

in two minds about,
slipping 2 survive past
Feeling 2 Much, streets flooded with fake Feeling II,
chickens wearing sandwich boards
showing shadows
u want 2b wearing a Mask 2 Survive 4 what
reason but 2 become 2real 4 u
to bear 2b unmasked as 4 the
benefit of Feeling I wearing a
Mask 4 Survive 2 Feelings I
2 Feel and 4 what reason unmasked
as Feeling II involved in a shadow
II deep 2 survive, formerly
known as its former self,
aroused in the interior of the ordeal,
2 real and too pulsating, and too
withheld,
moving past Dream whispering
to a uniformed ellipse,
and past the Chicken Who Wears a Mask
now disarmed and dragged into the grey square;
and past another, censored poetry,
and past the interruptions of inescapable struggle and
inescapable care;
and past Understanding in Hi Vis linking arms with graphic
regression,
and past the vision of freedom
filed down to its dark undercurrent,
and past the flap of skin setting impassively above the
murder capital,
in search of a Former Self, drifting through residual
perishable categories
in the suburbs of prairie fire, hail and drought,
beyond the crude heat haze of Mayor I nostalgia, in a world

with the fewest possible elements,
a few tangles of intense lines,
eating 2-4-1 Feeling Is behind
an empty stomach mask, 2 real 4 this doubled up world
2 survive; past all of this,
down an alleyway towards a clearing
where reality is crossed out,
past my tongue standing around
in your head,
just waiting for something to fucking happen,
ignoring the small voice that says look up,
past small retail,
past self-harm, past the maze
injected into poverty,
past the abandoned districts of tonal implication,
past mixed up people crawling on our spindle legs
over a collapsing ground line, with our enormous circular heads,
guilt flickering in them
in an acrid montage without interlocking parts,
with no catch-up strategy
and no end, processed into Feeling I on the spectrum of
Ashen Frost
Wearing a Mask 2 Kill
that the Headless Chicken would fucking
be killed 4, in the cartoon stockyard under the supervision of
Time whose Slogan is I Have No Beheaded Phantasm For You,
under the radicalised sky,
the grey squares on fire; the stick figures marching in the
street singing
we learned to draw ourselves,
then we learned to draw ourselves together
we learned to be clever,
then we learned not to be clever, whatever;
the counter-drives, the exploded call centres for a distressed

structuralism,
U & I Trimmings, Low Cost Tropical Food,
teenagers standing around,
the places we live in; look up,
above the piles of killed cops
stacked like firewood in the side street off Liteinyi Prospekt,
crayon fascism, water colour liberal democracy,
thought bubbles crashing like blimps
above the elastic skyscrapers, urban poverty in felt tip,
indescribable longing driven from the market by cheap UV
Cambodian Feeling I
Wearing a Failing II Mask Feeling I Mask
rippling through the Non-Vacuum
re-opening as a vendor of inner stick figure Mayor IIIs
preserved in jars,
clasping the nameless comedy lever
from an earlier life,
talking of nationalising Feeling II,
of clarity,
the shadow of the former self
cast in steel,
helpless love and fire and smoke,
of the Chicken, the Phantasm,
the Shadow, Take-Ur-Job,
the rich vein of the Former Self, not the Former National Self,
not Mr. Interior Minister eating a ragdoll,
but the straw people 2 die for,
in opposition to the growthless revolt of the talking head
grafted onto stunned silence;
talking of the fucking class enemy
standing around in the meadow lubricated
under the anaesthetic of reason, watching fascism
come up over the municipal swimming pool,
a dead sun illuminating the watercolour factory, pumping

crude Feeling I into the sky,
involving A Quality More Complex and More Open than Irony
shuttered in the collapsed magnetic grey economy of trial
and error,
stick figures selling Tragic Wing-Mirror Masks with a non-
stick tongue of flame 2 die 4
beneath the shadow of the skinless retail centre
stretched to the uttermost limit of Feeling III,
coming up in a structure with your principles burnt off,
feeling volatile and II, in a relationship with I,
in search of a new feeling, stuck in a dead form
or in a fenced up neighbourhood, half-awake,
clutching a thin strip of vitality, watching the shops
mature and then begin to rot, in a dead neighbourhood,
in a new form, in front of a fenced off feeling,
so fucking close now, though the strip thins out
across all of our reverses, and the skin grows
back over it: if I do not innovate I will not die,
but I can still see it, past the good old times,
the crude outlines of a failed revolt against
the Former National Self, Mr. Interior Minister,
the bread line of powerless Mayors who solve
nothing, the rootless seizure becoming randomly
accessible, midnight rolling out at the gas station
as the headless chicken clocks off and draws its
head back on. Try not to beat yourself up over it.
Start again.
Welcome stick figure, welcome puppet,
to a leaden scene of generative ambiguity;
reality doesn't have to be anything like this,
sheen of despair helps to forget about that.
Welcome surface effect including snow
and a draft torn open in the leaden streetlight.
Welcome gamut rips through the surface

to a sheen of sweat asks you to lay beneath it.
Welcome surface effect to a drift of rain
in a street anywhere, as if it mattered;
righteousness seen anywhere from a leaden keyhole
swirls through a surface effect including cauldron.
Welcome middle class, also a stick figure
stylised as the reality of defiance
while a sheen of defiance settles on it.
Unreality doesn't have to be anything like this,
most of the shadow confiscated by perspective.
Reality doesn't have to be anything like this,
stick figure gasps out or can't do perversity.
Rain lashed out needlessly at a shadow
impression implies this like ecstasy
sparks over a gap torn open by detail.
Go-to relentlessness it turns out is just an effect.
Anti-fascists have to tolerate frustration.
Draw blood from the conclusions or get their sweat kicked in.
Welcome Crude Teuton from the sheen of defiance,
to eroticise doubt flame contracts to a blip.
Welcome Moral Crusade Puppet from the sheen of defiance,
what's your opinion on how reality is manipulated.
Cold emptiness of streets stubbed out by generative ambiguity
seems like a blip lit unfaithfully by nihilism.
Welcome pretence of being overwhelmed,
nightly stubbed out bits of you get re-screened;
welcome AI Teuton running a ragdoll;
pore over the sheen lashing out through the streetlight
folded over inside can't do perversity or even gasp for it.
Past another exercise in sentimentalism.
Most of us want to be more than that,
but don't want to be nothing,
nothing is the backlight for the mirror in which
100% crouches and conceals the reflection of its nakedness;

what part of us wants to say is that we want to damage
change itself,
100% change trampled under foot by a flaming ragdoll
crying like a cartoon stick figure version of a puppet,
want to kick through the sheen of it doing a ragdoll
impersonation
on the way to those who told you that you used the feelings
wrong,
to kick through the sheen that was being used to prop up
the sky that should go over your head, if you have one,
and go out into the dark screaming
that if you don't
then why not
step out from under its shadow.

From At Close Range

[A]ny kind of freakish feelings better than no feelings at all

nothing is different now than it was 15 minutes, an hour ago
the situation is the same, the world is the same. nothing
has changed. my mother visiting a 'troubled teenager'
in say 2549 did not say anything, she just removed her hands,
one after the other, and placed them on the table.
it is not a real speech that I am giving. It is not a true speech.
It is not a beautiful speech I am giving. It is not a correct speech.
The factories where I grew up had stained glass in their windows,
we would look out through them at the theme park they
          were building,
it was called Dud Dud World, and soon we would all work
          in it forever,
off our nuts in its Social Services department, though it was
          rife with child sexual abuse,
and the managers all covered for one another

it is not

No one knows whether he will live or whether he will die,
everyone has a coin they can toss,
even the poorest of us.
Coins don't count for much,
your opinions don't count for much, either.
fifteen minutes ago,
an hour ago
I saw the theme park lights go off
I would've said it doesn't really matter

First peak (I)

Rainy night, downtown unknown heat it is
known to affect children and there is dim
sertraline of a light grey in them they are
white dirty little beaches, without change
we sat together by a dirty little hole in the
wall we bought nothing said nothing our
memories were gone our arms were gone
too brittle little faces like peaches we had
both smoked listening to the wartime music
unknown pink screaming downtown heat rain
UK garage from a thousand little holes
in the wall a rainy night a thousand dirty
white blimps a million yellow beaches

First peak (II)

Rainy night downtown unknown heat, it is
never too late here and there is always
a dirty little hole in the wall someone
smokes the skins of peaches are scattered
on the beach like discarded needles there are
indications for use printed on them
in sassy pink rings of heat drifts of smoke
through the roads a little something to eat
if you need it yellow NY-Tokyo
unknown screaming downtown wartime Flowers
Remix from a thousand streets a dirty
cab a person's heat on the seat say
it was eighty years ago another thousand holes

you are one of the ones we will not be able to bring back

you are one of the ones we will not be able to bring back
for whom they have refrigerated the parks in readiness
I would that they were colder still,

mediocre male desire such an easy distraction
there are only two kinds of love I know
you know this /

I know you know this. the stately
home turned into a house for abused teenagers
push your hands high if you feel it

one evening in December
I had an idea about how language is itself a kind of abuse

the woods behind it were so beautiful
you are one of the ones we will not be able to bring back

put your hands in the air

the hay bales are on fire again. we walk down to the shore
where the shattered skeleton lies slumped over the baby
grand piano amid the remains of the day's celebrations.
bullshitter's vomit streaked on my chinny chin chins. i pick
out a few old chords on the grand: the greenhouse walk-in
centre. a young mother in the lifts i was standing on the
stairs so as not to get too close i smiled and said hey there
in the dark the fire flies from wrist to wrist from cup to cup,
they are not like part of my life they are not like part of my
life and the doors slid shut. i wipe my mouth. i think the
skeleton's voice is weak as fuck. it sings like shit behind the
beat. its words don't mean a thing. it sounds like teenage
smoke rising over a village in january. a gratuitous flower
bed watched over by paedophile grocers. a neat little story
about class. it has a new pain in it. sweet as our facemasks
in the club if you feel it put your hands in the air if you feel
it the hay bales are on fire again we thought it was weak
af, like eating grey strawberries on the reddest night of the
year it has just enough sweetness in it. singing without a
microphone. its chin tilted up. its voice was weak af like in
all great art it makes us feel there is something boiling in the
world as the majority of us experience it with no degenerate
allegories no idiotic fantasias no dream material no visions
of how things might be nothing that looks impressive or
imposing just pain and desire obliterating everything in a
weak little voice like a pin dropping baby-o and it could be
playing in a shop somewhere it could be playing in a Co-op
and you wouldn't notice it rip away your heart in the way
only real art does. like talking to your children over Skype.
one of them shrinking its face gone like a skeleton's Singing

but no sounds coming out only light the baby grand the
remains of the night's celebrations the lake the fantasia and
our bodies on the ground in sulphurous null point shut the
fuck up blue as if on Skype in conversation, the zombie
slumped across the piano because like all great art from cup
to cup this one's got some ambiguity in it. a lil ambiguity.
and i put my hands in the water because i feel it dipshit
grey-blue strawberries bending just beneath its surface in a
song that seems so personal it gave one the feeling of being
taken into strictest confidence by another who needs so
intensely to 'tell it all' that each syllable turns in its sleep.
listen. listerine in the cabinets yellow light from the bulb we
thought it was weak af. and i heard something like violence
in it beaucoup pain and desire in it in a tiny weak voice like
hay bales on fire where the city meets the windless plains
and i heard a murdered note in it, and then another and was
like hey tiny weak voice stumbling along tarmac this is real
life you know like in real art you know with no way
of disguising constriction boredom complacency the things
you failed to fight for & no quick fixes either you either
make it sound good or you don't. 20¢ drinks at the bar. a
handful of boke grey strawberries the world as the majority
of us experience it with no allegories no fantasias just a
man pulling up saying get into the car with just enough
sweetness in it. in a tone that has nothing to do with what
the words say. listen

uneasy feelings nothing specific
unless a petal hit the ground
don't call me

that

don't call me that

looking back on things
a few provisional conclusions
teenage children should not sleep in the same room. The EU
Hysterical middle-class poetry doesn't even know
Can't feel anything except anger. at myself
solipsistic anger cut off from reality don't
care about the dead
pretence of sympathy for the dead worse than none at all
I feel none today so that is better

Hysterical middle class poetry sleeps in the same room
as unrecognisable reality, on some crushed glass

Anyone can harden. don't call me

05.05.20

do gooder (I)

in this country as nothing contains us I have no words
to describe how it can happen
in a circle, as its radius
extends, indefinitely. This is the most beautiful sound it is
        possible to make,
to do violence so long as it is personal, and beautiful
to whoever
it is as nameless in an a&e entrance as in any circle its
indefinite radius

its accusation is general I am alive
everything else is what culture is we can steal a purse on the
overground no one real is hurt by this
In this country it remains
nameless as Yves Saint Lauren will be nameless as every
        ibiza anthem extends
the radius
of that act, indefinitely,

I am only alive in the circle of that act
at its centre there is nothing except disbelief
disbelief is the most beautiful sound it is possible to make
it contains and completes
all other possibilities
and is the centre of all possibility.
I am alive everything else is what culture is

Lord Adonis
for c.h.

In the great floating network of orphanages and children's
centres I spotted them instantly, their innocent faces
walking into bright steam rising from itself alone I saw
them disappear into little bright pieces of glue and greasy
finger marks instead of eyes once thought beautiful.
deep poverty, pervasive drugs, obesity and anti-depressants
followed me, with bright red beaks and plumes
instead of eyes it is quite common for small sockets to leak with.
fuck around with phrases to understand this
world it is heat years away, there are no 'orphanages'
a single orange tree grows in its garden of pure time
the grass waves it is heat years away that splashes evenly.

quite commonly it is a person the victim knows,
and against that rising tide of filth the orange tree bursts into
the same things again pervasive drugs, obesity
surging into the minibus 'JD Sports bag' a moral 'glittering'
all over the minibus seats 'radiance' fades heat
years and intense blossoms to menthol, 'you' sexualise that
glittering inappropriately anyone in the minibus can see that
there are no 'orphanages' 'anti-depressants'
a single orange tree dies in its garden of pure time
white england is an orange grove,
walled off and 'glittering' there is a
minibus parked near it

driven by 'radiance' to a dark spot. & we become greasy
finger marks on its windows, the orange tree cracks
into disconnected images and phrases like nothing

'radiance' ever did to you in that minibus
could ever stop this made deep marks on my skin, which
in 'JD Sports bag' yellow and 'empty inhaler' blue
would unite obesity and falling rain crack
filth and sky in a single 'hurt' 'random'
'glittering' phrases nothing can tower and soak through
convulsively in cracks of 'radiance' phrases like
an ash glitters and 'towers of phrases' done in
empty inhaler white and the most obscene nicotine blue

would do anything in that minibus, for you,
disconnected images,
for whatever you do to 'radiance' is justified.
no glittering phrases can change that.
'a single orange tree, in a garden of pure time',
it is heat years away,
& realism is all words it don't know how to keep its mouth shut
the minibus has arrived.
inside
signs of a struggle there is another struggle
its signs also point inwards, and so on until the end of our lives.
fuck around with phrases till you understand this

The Inquiry In Its 4th Year

That truth is known instantly
as a lantern revolves in the market
briefly I am still standing
beneath that underpass, it shines
sticky as lanterns burn in
space lines of them stand quietly
screaming dark threads of them,
to a gallows across an estuary.
& what counts now is to be still,

and observant.

Since truth is a whip with no windows
gallows-red and shining briefly
liable to tear through us as lanterns
blink spaciousness and
dropping easily through that
quinquennial underpass it is
my baby gallows, across an estuary
your tasteful cream image my
screaming dark threads of them

our cladding

Advice Column

The Argument

The narrator, having undergone an affordable operation in the toilets of a McDonald's, is exposed to radiation from the flash of an airborne speech camera. Feeling their body undergoing a series of unwelcome changes, and in a state of severe mental perturbation, they venture through the streets of a city of many nail bars, in search of a route to the giant floating ambulance overhead, representing heaven, the need for injury as a proof of the depth and reality of experience, and the compulsion towards violent speed, in that order. This framing conceit established, the narrator explores the overshadowed city itself, where they encounter evidence of a civil war entering its final stages, conducted largely by means of flying transport vehicles given the name of Costas. As the physical symptoms of the accident increase in severity, a series of episodes and flashforwards shows the narrator receiving support in a respite centre in the ambulance itself; encountering the body of a pilot in a bathroom; and attempting to avoid the attentions of an internationally prominent human resources firm contracted to sweep up the mutants. Images of care and dependency prioritised. The floating nailbars and cafés shown in picturesque form, not as incident vehicles tearing through the sky, but instead as assorted shifting spots of coloured light: here, ideas of beauty and gratitude in the recognition of common humanity are re-asserted in the tone of sarcastic disbelief, which, in a world where the fact that anyone can take a shit in a McDonald's represents the final redoubt of universal social provision, is the only tone the narrator feels able to access in good faith. In a final attempt to reach the ambulance in time, the narrator passes upwards in the lifts of one of the city's few remaining tower blocks. Shapes are seen moving in a number of branded forensic tents, a council office is seen as if in a vision, and at last we stumble across a disorganized protest in the carpark of a Tribunal Services building. Feeling the changes to their body becoming at last irreversible, but no longer depressed, and with the negative symbolism of the ambulance sufficiently established, the narrator joins the protest, where along with its other participants they watch, in passive contemplation, as the all-overshadowing emergency vehicle is consumed by spectacular foliage from within. The story concludes with some advice on the broader implications of withholding information from a local authority.

Prefix

Float away down No snitch street, float away
    without let or pause
    dirty little secret street
We will have to rename
     everything
another rotten human interest story.

your hands your face your arms your life
    the road is long
    and has nothing in it
Run away from letters
     court injunctions,
No snitch street, headache, rain and shit.

The things I've recognised about myself,
     a McDonalds toilet,
A pit five miles long
    We must rename our
      body parts,
as we walk in the ambulance in silence.

Adult Social Services street. a lurid
     speech
     in a packed forensic tent.
I will never forget a single syllable
      everything
it made my body twist and float away

my tongue my hair my eyes my nails
    the bar so full,

           a voice, sweet
push through the crush of rising heat. Never
           trust
the state street, blank feelings, black-out drunk.

spill out on No snitch street, float away
           a children's centre
           a pit ten miles long.
Men come to disassemble the tent,
           from agencies,
with hernias, bad backs and shit

then spill out on No snitch street, drift away
           it is quiet now
           stay loyal
street I don't need to know a thing about
           instincts
Run away from intimacies,

admissions. what do you want, for the state to do it.
           Like a
             single syllable
just push the hernia back in,
           painlessly
beneath a hot latex sun, at night

you will always be able to rely on me
           Speech.
             plastic chair
street set-piece feelings
             all these
squares and circles walk through us

with sound systems, clarity, dreams and shit.

float away,
            down Never wait street,
ways of living. marxism, cold air, stations
            through which
nothing passes. the Bakers Union McStrike policy,

we're going to rename everything.
            Again.
            Euery thing.
two great lights. a McDonalds toilet
            court injunctions.
tell me yeah, how all this started

Advice Column

All our ideas are perfect images.
Cold storage city, the content of
a hernia. An idea hangs out of it,
The speech cameras flash over o

ur heads we dont worry about th
at its the Ambulance chasers wh-
ho will suffer it it's the ambulan
ce chasers in the Costa who will

start to mutate. flipped swelling
allegory i think solidarity is bea
utiful and will die in a park to p
rove it. frontline services let me

aning hang out of it theres no reason to comment its an ongoing
investigation. second-tier tribun
al clear milk in the sinks. Is this

my fingers itch. change nothing.
the cold tiles of colour, no wind
and the clear milk. Fuckers. dreams spat out have red in them a

Pink light fills the sky we could
all feel it spreading we can all b
e revived on the floor and go on
to lead an almost normal life, O

please can you hear yourself we
have no needs a see through ten-
t shines in the street, the light bl
ue of a burning refrigerator repr

esents violence like nobodys bu
siness. and we can all feel it spreading, beneath the ambulances
which will never descend, and i

n the chain cafés so many miles
from free childcare and training,
we can all feel it swelling in the
toilets at Mcdonalds, we can all

feel it falling and rising, yeah rising you heard we can all feel it
breathing. An idea hangs out of
it. All our ideas are found unres-

ponsive in a park by a dog-walk
er, the world is so beautiful just
give me your phone. a little gre-
en in the foreground like shit th

rough a letterbox. I'm not talkin
g to you, yeah, we can all feel it
twisting our ideas are all gone y
ellow light in the drop-in centre,

will never descend yeah as our i
deas as our images o wow as ou
r symbols flashing so gently. So
bright like clear milk we can all

feel it spreading. Stolen car radi-
o stolen vast lake, it is like floating in the foreground, the toilets˙
the carpark an idea hangs out of

push it back yeah, the landing th
e stairwell, o flipped swelling al
legory it's like nothin can hurt u
s not the ambulance not the cost-

as we can all feel it swelling. an
ambulance, a sky an all-night n-
ailbar just blinking. just circling
all our lives yeah any nailbar an

y image. a tile yeah a babywipe.
its like we're all going to just li-
e here on the floor yeah forever,
Singing songs about what we'll

do behind the dustbins, for a fiv-
er. You know how it is, vaguely
wet crimson shadow x leyhill O
pen prison, that kind of thing ye

ah, so what you going to do abo
It is the same wet on the tiles. a-
bleism. now wipe your lips. We
are everybody the toilets repres-

ent love, and the cessation of su
ffering. look up at the ambulanc
e, its credit suisse charity-do raf
fle like a stain on our crotch, ha

s no one ever told you how *ugly*
it is. & across the whole surface
of the earth, and at each altitude
we can all feel it speading we c-

an all feel it rising and falling w
e can all split in two on the tiles
in the toilets at McDonalds, and
scream o my god it's like dying

in a world with no scabs, with a
pin in our hearts o wow it's like
screaming *we're all blurring* w-
e're going to the mass rally this

evening o you should come to i-
n the aisle yeah, our court day's
approaching. fire escape with m
ain artery how come there are n

o rich people here in the brick f
ields it's snowing that's not real
ly the point anyway. moment w-
ith lips in an ideal world, like in

the case of a late-term pregnanc-
y its like dying in the lifts in a p-
ink semi-circle on our own in th
e toilets with our mouths closed

it's hurting close your eyes, step
into the streets. theres a burnt co
sta on its side, no ones paying m
e to say this in the shadowless b-

oats by the pastel nightshelter cr
ap like this is why Donald Trum
p got elected o wake up with the
phone ringing, now dry now yel-

low with a feeling like no one's
getting pinned down in a TV ro
om. it's about time someone sai
d something bathroom mirror ti

les wet promise its like somethi
ng none of us ever even dreame
d of on our teabreaks. Shitty litt
le 15 minute scraps of infinity y

eah it started in our stomachs, n
o no one made me do it yeah I s
uppose that its significant. Dyin
g high street with light rain like

Steel bats through a windscreen,
distinct ideas never hurt anyone
sometimes it feels like there's n
othing we can do about it. O go

get yourself an image of two un-
walled facilities three suns hanging over them we all walk throu
gh the checkpoints i had never s

een shadow. what you playing a
t. some more health & safety bu
llshit. access agreements you ca
n go on ahead we'll all slumped

outside the costa. We're all perf
we're all this sweetness without
end we're all beginning in the d
ark outside the clinic, We thoug

ught we saw it moving. a forensic tent a touch of local colour, y-
ellow light in the drop-in centre,
o look here is my real voice it is

the nails that go first and then th
e rest of the fingers. My other re
al voice is thin chants rising fro-
m the carpark, and flow through

our body in little perfect shavings of shadow forever o please h
ave you ever seen a shadow, half laughing half serious. Do you

look a cure, advertised from the
ambulance how perfect how beautiful it is it represents nothing.
All our ideas are perfect images

on its side just scrolling just blinking the speech cameras, flash
and will never descend. pauses,
o look here is my real voice it is

like we are all singing, Oh yeah,
this is what an elegy is its sweat
ing in an intake office representing struggle, yeah its sweating i-

n an intake office representing s-
truggle in our sweat and blood i-
n lungs and hearts and chests an
art of sweating in an Intake offi-

ce, representing struggle. patter-
dots of work. a grey corridor. A
its like we're all here, like holes
punched in metal we can all spe

ak in riddles Oh yeah huge grey
fire here's your image of freedo-
m oh my God look its waving fr
om the dark yellow rooftop, see

the world is so beautiful it has t
hese shelters and clinics yeah it
s all so exquisite you can feel it
breathing shallowly no one eve-

r leaves here. A thousand perfe
ct nail bars, always the same ta
steless symbols all our senses i
listen to all the time yeah it shit

s on your tribunal. beautiful lev
itating images don't you ever f
ucking touch them, pink foregr
ound of Nails where one of our

Security Officers will meet you.
scarred by it bright sky in every
last part of our body dont you e-
ver start to feel it at the Mandat

ory training. Its like we've all g
ot some soap and no one has sc
abies, there's no snitches on the
hotline Oh my god its so beauti

night rain on the roofs. Other sounds. pauses. its like no one got
eaten in the back of a uber right
its like we were all moving thro

gh the fences at calais Open wid-
e now like you didn't even fucki-
think we were edible. oh move o
n officer hows that lump in your

throat yeah lets all divide it with
a pin for eternity. yeah vast hum
an tragedy i am looking at you y
eah in the place where you're go

ing no one cares about essences.
burning sensation with a few pl
astic chairs in it, try not to stare
too deeply into the crowndale c-

entre all our senses are there an
d they all want appointments, t-
o die and be reborn on a sofa at
a friends house yeah you know

how it is in a bathroom with pieces of teeth and hair in it. A bur
ning sensation like no we didn't
do what you want to me, pink-f

aced manager outside a Human-
faced windmill I was standing i
n the corridor in the shape of an
animal with my hand against th

e handle to the door of the Prep
room. All our ideas are running
theyre all streaking in places al-
l our blackened tree stumps, all

our empty white landscapes the-
y all seem to be shrinking throu
gh the window at Costa o insan-
e fucking cameras, look our fin-

are swollen. & o we didnt see it
coming in the shallow pink wat
er in the car in the elevator in a-
nything representing motion yo

u know who I mean behind a gr
ey plastic curtain. you're still th-
same person. everything overgr
own can you see the recruitmen

t centre searchlights. this is our
life We clean away its sick and
wipe its mouth a thousand time
s yeah not one blade of grass y

eah not one note out of place. it'
s like we all lay still with our ba
cks upon the Lino, waiting for s
ome screw to come from Social

Services. Blinking night of cele
brities drowned in all their pool
s yeah. Harm not one hair upon
their hearts stay not your hand i

live for, pin money. slinking gut
less swirling image of a corrido-
r we row frantically, to the very
end of our ideas, there is nothin

All our ideas of perfect images,
slight darkness at the knee we l
ook up at the lights all the time,
& the rain coming down so ope

nly. a nailbar, just joyriding, by
the thin white canals. A library.
A Costa docking in the ambulance like a syllable in our throat

we will never tell them O total,
total health and safety incident,
we will never tell them, even a
single thing picked out by the s

ickly yellow searchlight of that
pret on the highstreet will wither and will wither in our throat.
clear rain, in rhythm with the h-

eart, in those toilets to which w
e return, and where we will nev
er die, fall softly and darkly. At
noon a little grey figure dances,

& seems partly swollen, at night.
& how empty the lights how empty they seem, and O wow, how
the clouds move across them. w

hatever. hired models by the bu
rning refrigerator crouch Move
On Officers from the Local Au
thority crouch Ghosts from our

past lives and videos, crouch. st
ab yourselves with a pin suck y-
our bellies right in, yeah ascend
on a cross of two matchsticks ta

da. I love everyone, we all do, i
ts in our nature to love, O bitter-
ness its over how sweet is the a
ir now never die in a taxi never

Go hungry for an hour. It is like
it's nothing to do with you yeah
I know its cool and rain cools o-
n our skin and the mind contain

s its own body. flick knife in a s
auna, filthy as a gov office slick
split me down the middle music
i see pink nail bars forever yeah

pink nails bars that do not bend
nor snap. We wipe their lips a t
hin rain answers, Yeah, I know
a thousand times. inside the car

see costas hijacked, burning, pi
nk images they never die in flat
s like us they never die. there is
always something waiting at th

e end of the carriageway, perfec
tly lit Virgin forensic tent i thou
ght we was just talking all slick
yeah like music no i don't rate t

he service. tiny cream intensive
care unit night after night this n
ight and the next yeah like pink
nailbars they burn for a momen-

t in offices you distort my body
Alright. We can all die in taxis,
We can all paint symbols on th-
e walls of certain temples. Dea

Watching red mist drank deepl-
y by the Assessment vehicle w-
indow. All of the little parasols
on the beach All these paracete

mol, some blood spots on your
collar yeah this life the white o-
f fingernails. and wipe its mou
th. and wipe its lips. and touch

its hair yeah help it dress. leave,
detention guidance GUM clinic
miles from anywhere how did t
his happen I thought we were fr

Its like they throw us in vans an
d we only grow stronger golden
smoking city of Mandatory Trai
ning, how bright shine your nail

bars oh flow through our bodies
do what you want to me in shelt
ers and clinics there has never b
een limits let's all stand on the j

etty, like we've never seen shad
e yeah like no one can hurt us. I
ts like We can all stand together
in motorway services singing so

ngs about the transcript from ou
r last call to the HelpCentre thic
kening at the edges feeling, pov
erty porn body language it does

nothing for me yeah i can see it
mouthing somethings changing.
4 previous worlds from the mat
ernity ward window 2 Governa

nce Officers in the pink light of
this landscape. How bright shin
e your nails in the floating, swo
llen waiting room, everything h

ere is beautiful where our Gove
rnance officers will meet you. a
cause of death porn body thicke
ning into poverty. we all love ev

eryone we all have long red nai
ls and lips like pins, and the Su
n has gone you wipe our mouth
you comb our hair, you watch t

he costas lights come on, one b
y one, and never die in flats lik-
e us. Representing class like us.
pink and cocoa yeah like us, yo

u never die. small pink flag that,
Free Wifi from the legs down. c
elebs in the foreground here are
some microwave meals represe-

nting poetry. Yellow morning li
ght sticky heat shared bathroom
no sound in our mouths no keys
All our ideas are perfect images

came to study as nurses its a ple
asure boat in flames, I feel the s
ame, that theres no limits, like a
clinic, for every bruise on every

body red morning light pink hai
this is what im talking about, in
a bathroom of sick symbols this
is what we're feeling. windows,

of the microwave. Waves of na
usea waves of hope, it's a pleas
ure fire escape it's a pleasure m
icrowave, dumped in the car pa

rk like an idea this is what we'r
e trying to say there's no sound
system here theres a human bod
y in a bathroom in a tiny pink c

osta stand up yeah and say it in
a thousand pink nailbars radian
t pink like we're puking there's
a burning refrigerator, all golde

n vomit on our baking lips a rep
etition. ideas never snitch never
ending costa walls soundless cr
owns of grease never scab neve

r never, though the whole world
may and the stars, and the buses,
and the trams yeah, and everythi
ng representing motion never go

back into that bathroom never le
t me hear that word upon my lip
s. still image. like a clinic. hows
about you just turn around, keep

and the lifts. Only lips travel up.
in the office, we can all lick our
lips we can all look out on open
heart surgery city see its I.T dep

ts. twist in the office I raised my
hand before my face its twisting
fingers will not change only pill
s will slow their changing o god

never scab hot disinfectant we e
at that raw, hot sticky image the
thermometers of the prison cant
een represent brightness itself it

s sudden rapture of spirit. Fat pi
g white man with a house in Ch
elsea it is brightness itself repre
sented like everything denied to

us it is flowing through our bod
ies during mandatory testing its
lips its veins its six silhouetted
senses, oh my god yeah its nam

e written on a badge with a biro.
who wrote you off. stool sample
tender grasses, raid our flats our
hearts arent drinking. ambiguou

s planets. Always looking down
on us. we raise our hands to our
faces keyed car the faintest blue
costas there is never much to sa

y collapsed ceiling, Vetting and
barring we lay motionless, as if
activists in their 20s and 30s pu
shing prams yeah we lay deligh-

tfully still in our thousands, in t
he concentration ambulance bri
ght blue costas pumping like th
e heart do nothing for us. Make

do with that, scab english planets who a pin could deflate. You
look down on us, don't fucking
deep breaths there is a loyal sta

r it is always out it makes us ill,
in a library together like thousa
a thin rain wakes us in our beds
again, all these Costas dying in

the streets again hired models l-
ie face down again yeah split m
e do you down the middle musi
c on our lips again again a thou

sand times, get up, this life thes
e thousand lips this golden blac-
k red mist forever yeah. five ne-
w sport centres they are more t-

han distinct they are like pins s-
tuds of light o bright and dying
flipped incident vehicle we can
all feel it swelling in the toilets

at McDonalds we can all see it
twisting we can all split in two
and drift across the car park. fluorescent drops of rain bruises

who are you a dog-walker o wa
sh me wipe away our ideas, trashed all trashed we walk like ai
r bruises us. Beneath the shado-

w of an Ambulance, that cannot
be prevented & will never descend, we will float into the lobby
Some story about how he was a

represent immediacy the cold, c
hoking air of an air-conditioned
space where nothing is ever ach
ieved for us o yeah nothing rain-

bruises on our skin. o costa inci
dent vehicle, destroyed by light,
we can all avoid windows we c
an, all sit on swivel chairs from

8 in the morning, singing songs
about whats growing where our
fingers used to be, dont you see,
the world is beautiful it's got al

l these millions of cubicles its g
ot crimes on CCTV yeah who c
ares it's fucking floating. o disa
ppearing nailbars representing s-

pace, there is never much to say.
hard wind where the tribunal wi
ll be held for each thing there is,
Get the fuck out of our lives ple

ase get the green out of the foreground wash our bodies make u
s incidental yeah, inject that cro
let us lie here, unresponsive, lig

ht our faces like hired models, s
tick some tubes into our bodies,
We can all come to life, we can
all remember something useless

from the hour of unpaid training
A riot in the ambulance. On our
knees you see a city falling emb
ers falling down our faces order

your burger dickhead, we dont h
on the park bench we saw something growing from our chest, an
ambulance blocks out the suns o

up-to-date information, it is so g
ood to be alive, lets chain oursel
ves to the doors of all the poorly
attended committees, golden vo-

mit silver faeces in a transparent
c-wing Costa why don't we do s-
omething. close your eyes, imag
ine the embers falling in a counc

il office. in silver-pink our throa
ts lips & pores bulge beneath ou
nces of thick, stinking crown. re
presentations of crisis centres th

rong the air like blown leaves, o
muesli types, mods in ski masks
Give us help and assistance never open your eyes, show us how

to fill out the forms in the librar
y together like we care for each
other Adecco sniffer dogs, gent
ly burning we are not sick we a

che, and swell inside those grey
dots. squat the lot. letters in a p
lastic bag this smell of sick this
abdication o swim in happiness

put our name down, wipe our b
eating hearts with disinfectants,
you never know they might ins-
pect it Adecco beach inside the

ambulance there is no sea thoug
h only bodies. the Sick, the Pill,
the Dole. Pornographic images,
they hang in the corridor like p-

ink planets shine through the m-
esh fence of the exquisite Costa
checkpoint. we press our palms
through the links a calm feeling

like everything ever denied to u
s is lying in the foreground. silver streaks its face a shower of a-
ttributes swims in happiness. O,

hired models we are, and in the
toilets of McDonalds can never
die, though our hands may turn
to pulp in our gloves and our m

ouths may be stuffed with pills,
to slow their changing. flash ba
stard, even your mind is a scab,
darkening green withdraws, for

no reason you laugh in our faces
like the voice laughs. last image.
never tell the council how beautiful are these stains on our crotc-

h these mugshots car thieves dream of. Race to the bottom of o
anything at all we can all live li
ttle shadows play across our lip

s and palms yeah never tell the-
m we can all see forever they'll
think its a nice little earner they
Pink mist drifts, in the car park.

never tell the council how beautiful is the bright flash of polishe
d steel it introduces. drain that o
ut. stupid words oh stupid ideas,

One day I met him on the fire escape the costas stretch away west of the garden like bright stain
ed glass we will never see shatt-

ered we will never see a bright s
ilver pool upon the staircase, strange lights they are the color of
do not snitch & we all sat, so lo-

vingly, in light incident vehicles,
rain comes from the trees do not
whisper in my ear flat cold sea o
nly the police station xmas party

could match you for spiritual de
pth x emotional intensity. Last i
heard image, indivisible images
say that again yeah and I'll be s

in court. walk on water, its baby
wipes we need, its the bodies of
huge animals washed up beneat-
h the saloon lights like small na-

ked figures in a library who nev
er snitch yeah never bend who'l
l never blink o orange sea no ca
sh machine is it always o is it al

ways o is it always, like this it i
s. I never met him never saw hi-
s fingers twisting, & that star w
ill never make us will never ma

ke us ill. this all began with pea-
ceful moments in a newsagents,
baby pink adecco searchlights t
hin fluourescent rain, flashing p

lastic all-night forensic tents we
drive for days, to the very end o
keyworkers do your homework,
it is not about you we can all be

found unresponsive in the toilet.
This all began with silver vomit
on our peeling lips, an orange s-
ea too beautiful to mention. nev

er tell the council all night flowers grow in the ambulance high
above the earth. where there once were costas. close your eyes,

imagine a carpark with no soundsystem, embers falling. candle-
lit emblem of employee loyalty,
you who cry out with joy like u

are never to descend, in the toilets at McDonalds an image wait
s for you forever it must necess-
arily be infinite, like a total pigs-

sty in woolwich that no sprinkle-
rs could ever alleviate o my god,
so many miles from free childca
re and training we all see the sig

ns yeah o we all see the sinks in
the distance, we can all feel it s-
welling, a little green in the fore
ground like a vast orange sea. O

open me please, the capitalists a
re all globalists the world is just
an alibi, the shelter hotline rings
forever pink forever sweet yeah,

Squat the grey fluourescent rain.
there are no rich people here. in
a carpark, with no soundsystem,
we all arrive together wet and b-

ruises all our bodies, fresh from,
pink nailbars our nails will neve
r. scratch this out. we arrive together. all our ideas are perfect b-

roken fingers, we can only hold
these flares with them. These. a
flower grows over an ambulanc
e in the air. the black medulla o

f the red tulip. costas pour from
its escape hatches in little perfect shavings of coloured shadow,
dickhead adecco flowers suitab-

le for any occasion shatter its wi
ndows oh wow how spectacular
ice creeps across the lake, like a
bbc accent kids home charity do

gala we are never found dead, a
nd will never tell the council ho
w beautiful it is in the carpark a
t night we can all watch the am-

bulance sinking into the Oceans,
we can all split in two we can al
l come to life in the taxi to the h
ospital, with pink nailbars in the

distance. Do what u want to me,
All our images are perfect ideas.
just don't engage with the cunts,
the more you engage with them,

the more they fuck you over. O,
tremendous stillness of what grows from our chest, a deckchair
has been placed here representi-

ng struggle, from the nailbars w
indswept and kept empty by the
nature of things we will emerge,
stronger than we were we will s

it in a plastic chair, yeah. and do
the crossword like lovers. we ha
ve hair on our lips; will never tell the council how beautiful it is,

how exquisite. never scab never

* * *

75

High Volume Bulk

Elegy

i.

I hurt myself in order to think clearly
but do not. And what is here,
darkening, is not early enough
to say. How fucked up, how cool
to be changed beyond recognition.
I think that you were
afraid of touching
like me;
the fear of being found disgusting
given names like tenderness or
moderation.
And now I fear that my desire
for solidarity is too thin.
Does the question
come down
to whether it is necessary
to hurt
people?
The equation of loving them and hurting them
is so deep in me,
I feel like I have to
rip it out from my life,
and the desire to do violence to it returns me to
where I started: the compensatory routine
of demonstrative self-harm as
the alternative to direct experience of
passion that will hurt whatever has
already been constituted.
Say it at least, stop trying to hide it from yourself.

If you hide it then you kill yourself.
Stop telling yourself
that excessive feeling will wound those to whom you display it,
that they will be harmed if you appear before
them sick and naked or loving or dead;
it is only your sickness and nakedness
that you are protecting yourself against.
Because when I hurt myself I am trying
to show that I am
capable of love, but
I take the love upon myself,
that I can bear the pain alone;
a towel placed against the bottom of the door
in the theatre of conscious uncoupling.
How fucked up, how cool,
to be recognised beyond change.

And then the frustration comes back in
like teenagers lying together on a bed,
wanting so much to touch
one another, or do
another line, though
the light is coming in through
the curtain and we are tired and can no
longer pretend not to notice it.
And that I haven't felt anger
yet or anything more
than a stupid, intermittent sadness
is predictable. There is
no point in trying to do too much at once.
And I loved you all so much,
so dumbly and so intensely,
and was so happy to be surrounded
by you and to be taught, slowly

that it didn't have to hurt for us to love one another,

though

the tightrope evaporates.

Leaving no wound.

And not in conclusion, David,

you are

ii.

you who
were so kind,
and calm
with us;

may the air
be kind
and calm
to you.

FWL

In one scene we both lie awake in the boat the sky is still 0
there are no thoughts in our heads water rocks against its
side like any night in which we lay awake in bed the taste of
cigs inside my mouth will not abate I reach into the blister
water and watch my nails come off like little barques, like

firebrands in the dark. They drift away. The sky is 1. The
sky is one huge class struggle Music mcdonald's the romford
rd a year two years ago the sky was 1 & on the 2nd or
3rd floor of almost every building on that street there was
a solicitor's office and in the solicitor's office a window a
filthy window that hasn't been cleaned since I don't know
and a sign saying Immigration Money Laundering etc. and
from it you could see darkly through the grey glass greasy
exhaust soot you could see thousands of them all joined
together in irrepressible circuit their colours muted sombre
and without expressive potential thousands of them gardens
joined by the most exquisite cast iron bridges fountains
& flyovers and in every second one of them you could see
in outline a lake a tiny grey lake always the same one you
knew its name it was called fucking wow lake and the little
boats that sailed on them were almost invisible dark streaks
against the glass and the little people that ache in them you
couldn't see at all how they dangle their hands in the blister
water so that one by one on each of their perfect fingers the
nail comes away like a little barque, a firebrand in the dark.
and you can also see a bus-stop with a Missguided advert
that someone has drawn a burka on.

CHAMPAGNE
(for SB)

> *The most Pathetic poem is small people on fire.*
> *—Frances Kruk*

A pleasure steamer sinks on the river.
there is no map of this place its streets look deserted

I have no thoughts in my head
the champagne is undrinkable tiny broken things swim in it
Washing lines items of clothing
the champagne is undrinkable it is boiling A skeleton dances
And we wave from the wheelhouse
as the sky splits in two like always, like always
I am too fucking impatient

A pleasure steamer sinks on the river
The canapes are rotten we're smirking
there's a flower in my mouth it is cooling
the champagne has a skin
a thought comes in my head a skeleton
and on the shore tiny broken things wave back
dark golden things by the washing lines
beneath a sky split in two, like always
don't tell me,

I know what you think.
things that twist as they burn
The skeleton opening its mouth
we suck on its lips till they're bleeding Young floating
people
-
on its lips, till they split like the sky splits,
like always. You say you just have
a feeling Fuck your feeling,
the champagne the music the river Thames in the 80s

was warm and forgiving, we could breathe under its surface
A thin crack ran through the earth
and the colour of blood on a sheet could be blue then
a flower in your mouth always burned then
all these thoughts

the music the champagne the screaming from Battersea
Power Station, in the 80s/
(so soft and arousing, O young people
the bottom of the river / so warm
and the music the champagne

the dancing the bodies all moving / the mud in our lungs
white splitting, like petals, in the morning
with our body cameras on, all filming these thoughts In our
heads
(A thin crack
and a single vague feeling
(fuck your feeling / a court telephone screaming
It is the Thames, in the 80s,
a string Broken things are all golden they blew
one another

all moving, all dancing and warm and forgiving
a pleasure steamer sinks on the river. the Thames in silence
not snow but a new kind/
flaming, as we wave from the wheelhouse
a pinch of grey ash in your mouth, where the flower used to be
O flower beds and body cameras, are you filming
It is dancing it is songs it is black sweat on our faces
it is mediocrity and boredom it's the papers each morning
it is your healthy new year's resolution.

Here is a world I accept it.
In the streets the people open their doors, and drown on
          their doorsteps.
The river looks calm and unbroken. It is the 80s.
In the cocktail lounges, surrounded by rubble for as far as
          the eye can see
all the air is pumped out and replaced with our filth

and one by one the Officers arrive and start thinking, and
          like planes falling towards the earth
like millions of tumbling white planes
their thoughts land in the poorer parts of our cities and are
          the source of a predictable sexual excitement.
All disasters announced years before they happen

Everyone knows it's necessary to maintain business confidence.
Drink up your drink it's going cold Young floating people
dark golden broken things
years will go by and no one will mention / this
and a silence will grow like the revolting skin on the surface
          of their champagne
a thick, stinking silence Machine silence they will blanch
          and find themselves unable to peel away
O Dark golden broken things
our Officers are all dead they are slumped in their horrible
          armchairs
Their thoughts in your heads are all starving,

they look like skeletons On skinned moons.
A passing reference to epilepsy
and the river looks calm now (like skeletons
Fuck your feeling. Warm and forgiving
and the washing lines, the shadows, so cool then
the music and champagne
A thin crack through the earth
All the Officers are rotting their fingernails still grow in
          bright waves though
O Young

Floating broken things, who swam
from the boat All singing and burning towards the cocktail
lounges / a thought swims

in your head a thin wave overcomes it /
a skeleton surfaces
(thin cracks and doorsteps and lovely old radiation/
a new wave of
Champagne and shadow and
we were happy together
music and

Swim faster
The cocktail lounge is burning
We were happy together, our hands were cut off
The universe has a little fence and a window
our body cameras are turned on
caught it all
And on the train home each night we are troubled by the
      same thought
(a skeleton pushes through the carriage A wave rises to
swallow it
O swim faster,

We were happy together, our hands were cut off
And on the train home we bang them on the tables, /
sing faster
we were happy together, our hands were cut off / we Swim
      faster that way /
We imagined ourselves naked In December / as dead nails grow
across rivers / and In tents / How beautiful
(how 'intense'
Name the people you love
Cut their hands off

in the 80s
(they will come away easily
And on the train home together And at the bottom of the river

In Berghaus and Eurohike in bright waves
swim faster sing faster / Bang your stumps on the table your
      stumps
in the streets in the houses
all singing all moving and dancing
and warm and forgiving
in bright waves

together. All beaten Together. Fuck your feeling, together.
and the music and the warmth of the living

For J.H.P.

I

i went to the place we became nothing.
there was a lagoon there. there were two.
we stayed awake when there was nothing

to do. 24.02 In the pelvis. Waiting on report. Today. 27.02.
rooms filled by those waiting for transplants
29.03 new bones of cormorants and flowers

the TV left on in the struggle room
Never fucking trust anyone in institutions.
Ignore parliamentary politics.

Stones of flowers and cement.

II

I couldn't care less if he
gets six
a few stars.
ix
still breathing
European art self
5 flowers
I said, you haven't
never in
the bed flag
I wore, gutters all
screaming and
ix
like vague stamens no
trainers / like half a city in it.

III

none of this has anything to do with manysidedness. The
politics I'm interested is about KNOWLEDGE, as in,
the practical and specialised understanding that anyone
needs in order to defend themselves against forces that are
fundamentally hostile to them. It's a form of understanding
despised by the whole personality-defining regime of
opinion about the 'representative'/oligarchic element of
the state, if only for the ignorant and finally self-defeating
reason that it isn't 'universal'; and its bearers are for the
most despised PEOPLE, which is to say anyone whose
knowledge is for the most part not so much personality-
defining as it is economically and professionally obligatory.

Think shelf stackers and nuclear physicists. An art that defines politics like this expands the domain of what it means to defend ourselves by reducing the domain of knowledge that only exists to be used against us. The tygers of wrath are still wiser than the horses of instruction, but they now snarl around an infinitely larger territory, with the same Imperial limits as industrial agriculture, the botched Deliveroo flotation and genomic modification. All the present-day Urizens crouching over their stupid little compass.

Everyone who is alive today is faced with the task either of learning Latin or burning down a courtroom. Poetry has no privileges but the privilege of doing both. "I learn to fight" means something else the second time you read it.

From At Close Range

in drenched aluminium

We change into clean clothes without meaning
became more clear about what we wanted an impermanent strange burned look
having nothing to do with intensity

and in the Travelodge the

animals are awake. their bodies are restored along with their minds
and the unique aspects of their personalities as they shower togeth
er in the sunlit hotel room we watch blood move through their lim-
bs in bashful calm motions like smoke from an oilwell, bright and

without shame

it passes silently without shadow of fragility degeneration or death
masquerading as insight it is beautiful clear blood it does not boil i
t need not boil all its phrases are completed in each motion all note-
s are driven to their ultimate values the animals cry out with delight

as blood

is something everyone can recognise as beauty strength power are
things that everyone sees and understands clearly with two very o-
bvious distinct meanings soaking through our jeans through cynic
isms thin cries 's nameless beautiful clear cries as ultimate values

whatever

If someone had given him antidepressants he'd still be around. any
bloodlit hotel room would do the animals freshly resurrected woul-

d shower we would use an intimate style of address it need not boil if it were to boil the tone of their cries would change I wanted th-

I needed them

to cry out in delight the blood would pass through their bodies and converge toward one point the hotel rooms strange burned look an address in wembley bloodlit by two translucent animals, returning I would fail to keep this simple strange burned room alive without

forget it

We change into clean clothes without meaning became more clear about what we wanted an impermanent str-ange burned look having nothing to do with reality

do gooder (II)
on the occasion of trump's speech on the
white house south lawn

We gather expectantly on another lawn
Oct. 2020, Ashford, Kent.
how fluent and beautiful the lorry park any of us could leap
        into,
blue and leaving a blackened say sibilant scar.
fake 'identity politics' whatever

is burnt vanishes, everything unbelievably bate fragmentary
and nonsensical departs from this world. And
isn't it curious, that any of us could leap into
Ashford, Kent's open pit, unbelievably blue and numb
a smatter of suns and thin meteors run

like sticky mud through gaps, the clouds
unbelievably small and hard bounce their
disproportionate and formless ass.
the fuck is 'acceptability' anyway
burnt vanishes loves away, the park studded

with perfect storms, as any of us could say sibilant
stays forever in the perfect studded away
bounces 'acceptability'. & we will protect one another,
against all vile winds of morality
red leaves in the thin branches and everything

they try to do to you will bounce off like metal
spring/summer Prada rains against the window pane
smashes through calmly, and everything they say

will bounce colourlessly to the edge of our
mind titillated uniformed light vehicles and

drop away from that, like Oct. 2019, Grays, Essex,
as deformed vile gaps in reality open
their mouths, bounce and smash meaning
on the edge of acceptability where nothing can hurt us
and all the beautiful things we think fuck, everything

they say to you or imagine they feel can bounce off like thin
metal sheets on the edge of our island
like everything they said unbelievably
numb smatters, like
sticky mud through gaps

and the clouds, unbelievably small and hard,
bounce their pointless ass.
everything disproportionately formless, bate and nonsensical
departs
from this world, let the earth fall from its axis

we will protect one another, from all the things we said
think feel, fuck, everything
even our batest sensations
like what the fuck is this anyway
will bounce away burning blue and vanish
equally in that unbelievably small and hard sea

as if they were as unbearably beautiful
blue and numb as the disproportionately beautiful and
unprotected people who died in that lorry on 23 October
and we are able to know the difference between victims and
            perpetrators
and we are able to see why they are reversed

Let us describe how they went. In late December south
through Bow on the A12. It was a very cold night and the
different scales of the city press up against the rolled-up
windows of a thousand nasty hatchbacks screaming in
and out beneath giant STAY AT HOME signs like 1,000
speeding fuck yous. I pull at the hem of my hood, try to get
it to cover my face. Big Yellow Storages and cement mixing
facilities stumble by; traffic reports crackle on the radio;
a bright 3/4 moon splits the top of the windscreen, and
we head down the A2 towards Dartford, the Xmas lights
flashing from the fronts of whitewashed semi-detached
homes, Purfleet to north of us along the other side of the
Thames, and an immense glass emptiness spreads before
us, perfectly flat and unresponsive, blacked out under the
attentive light of the moon, and absorbing and recycling
that light; and I wasn't even listening anymore but I thought
I heard you saying *that's a park*

No drama

i.

so what do you think beauty is? being stabbed to
death in a park? being suffocated in the back of a lorry?
being abused in a care home?
what kind of questions are those anyway.
when things get harder people who fuck themselves up
for consolation

start to die, we're supposed to be able to say it like we learned
something, I dont even care how it sounds
anymore
it's the end of the year, I'm going to
'explain'
the poems I've written because i can't

leave them be and have to keep picking at them like scabs
It's the only thing I've learned about myself, the tyrannical
            insistence
of the urge to make sense of things
which is as obstinate as the desire to fuck yourself
up & block everything out which is the inverse of it
its twin. two kinds of tyranny both of which

screams of feedback
stop talking like this.
anyway, in august of this year I wrote 2 poems.
one of them was a sonnet about the lives of US anti-racist
protesters
whose eyes were shot out by police in american cities
which i worked on for a day or two and then deleted in disgust.

the other started out as a description of a picture
of two women dancing with sparklers
in a park in wembley
before morphing into an inscrutable parable about 2
delicate, transparent animals showering together in a hotel
        room who cry out in delight,
dissolve and are reborn
only to repeat the same cycle again and again, for all time

I'd been reading milton that month, & when i was done
i realised i'd involuntarily reproduced this idea of
eden as a transient space
of human sexual fulfillment and togetherness
that i was fixated on the extreme delicacy of that state and
        that something was attaching it in my mind
to the image of those sisters who a few hours later

would lose their lives violently,
& I accepted that connection & never considered until
months later
that the animals might also be eyes
sacks of purposeless fluid blown out of the human skull
by beanbag rounds or rubber bullets.
or the 40 people found dead in a lorry in essex.

in the end I wanted these poems to be more inarticulate
than me, but also more loyal
I thought that a cursory understanding
of arterial roads was more important
than even our most advanced political demands,
and i couldn't care less who thinks that sounds reactionary

the constant interchange of feelings

of extreme violence and the need for intimacy
is just a reality
in me, like the unwanted associations that develop in
our heads:
there's no reason to be afraid of it

and as the wound in the leg of
the heroin user by the cash machine
is healed by the reality of our translucent and
delighted bodies,
& all of this shit that i never would have believed to
be possible
continues, all i really have left to say to you is
i need you to know

ii.

this is how it goes: all those words and images are beautiful.
and all the words and images retrieved from phones at
the bottom of ponds and from airtight containers all their
words for protection and assistance all their images of the
simple pleasure of being together in a park in west london
has been like my whole I don't know I guess my whole
goddamn 'theme' has been the time it took them to be seen
you know and all the space around them and the whole
weight of that body of water which I have felt as clearly as
anything I have felt or believed can be retrieved from me
along with the darkness heat and shape of those containers,
like a song off somebodys phone. so don't talk to me about
words you know phones are more beautiful than words
their images are more real and the music that comes off
them is crisper & more complete they contain coldness and
the heat of containers & even the weight of them is real
and what is scraped from them is real and everything i'm
saying to you is so obvious its so bate, phones are more
beautiful than words the most beautiful are at the bottom
of ponds and in airtight containers they contain words and
images come off them like music like heat from any body in
this world and each of them combines with the other you
know like everything I have felt and believed and we can
see into them everything can be retrieved from them even
the weight and the heat they contain and the wind through
the airtight containers that speaks clearly to me about what
has been, and will be like I don't know a Samsung Galaxy
or something, and this has been pretty much my whole
goddamn theme cant you see it's like everything I have felt
and believed and all the shoppers passing by and the
cordons on the ground with the nos canisters and used

sparklers is just scenery and all that stupid shit we say is so bate and so obvious. don't you see. the parks will be like screens, they will show everything that has been and will be, and we will walk in them in bare feet to stop the dumb shit that we said from appearing like paths behind us. and when we arrive it will be night, and the pond will seem more beautiful than seas, and the phone at its bottom more beautiful than words which float effortlessly across oceans. so dont speak to me about messages in bottles. every day i wake up, dont understand why i am alive, dont give a shit about the audience of the future. & in my memory there is no future only the audience that wasnt there & in my future there is no memory only the audience that wants to hear it. so no drama: it's time to go now, there are people following us along the paths, everything i have felt and believed has been forced into words into all these airtight containers i dont even want to use anymore. let the others deal with the bottles. the wind's picking up now, the bins are overflowing everything we said every last one of those words has a phone at its bottom and everything we felt and believed speaks on those phones like there is no future and everything will pass away like music off a phone or like flames in parked vehicles until nothing remains but airtight containers used sparklers and empty bottles strewn on the ground dumb symbols for all that stupid shit we say which floats away as everything we felt we believed says no, there wont be a future, and even if there is one we seen it already along with everything that has been and could be, and it can be said in just a few words i don't even want to use anymore. can you see. all the paths are disappearing, theyre sinking back into the ponds, the parks are shutting down. in the distance the arches of wembley stadium are lit by this low closing screen light. everyone is here now. T2 feat. Jodie coming up from the ground. all the stars bursting out.

and listen there are so many things i used to believe, and so many things i wanted to make true. But every word of it was said into a phone, and the phone was thrown into a pond, and the pond was cordoned off with tape in a park, and the park has gone back inside the words, to sleep in them, between their layers. let it go. sweet dreams. we can speak on the phone. everything will be its opposite. our beliefs are entirely unharmed, I won't tell you where they are. all these surprising moments of clarity. so many things

Halve Life

& every morning I get up and inject the state into my arm
and listen to the children singing in the nursery

the world is only ten years old
when the youth centres re-open the emptiness inside them

falls in the sea
at a hundred miles an hour we are its ceiling

& we have everything to live
for a hundred wild tubes from the mouth the ears and the anus

as the brains walk through the hearts
snow theme parks burn to the ground at a hundred miles'
        distance

all interior life at a hundred miles an hour
& every morning I get up their voices sound a little bit deeper

Letter to Sophie

Dear Sophie,

I don't really know what to write except a kind of report. I've barely written anything this year, the urge hasn't left me but I haven't known what to say. When I think about 'politics' I see nothing except a long trail of repression: Kazakhstan, Burma (teenagers with anti-fascist logos on their clothes run over by police vehicles), Hong Kong, China (massive nationalist inertia), Belorussia, France… a carnival of state reaction, activists killed, disappeared, tortured, exiled to the 'global cities' where they rot away doing nothing alongside all of the other members of the middle class with their laptops and language skills and documentary film projects and basic sexual anxieties (remember 'networked individuals'?), oppositional poets shot in the streets or left to die of respiratory diseases in under-equipped hospitals, basically the most intense state violence you can imagine, everywhere, in every country where people dared to come out into the street; and if you have the privilege of living in the US or the United Kingdom then things are the same but the Tiananmens are microdosed, the protestors get run over by personal trainers in SUVs instead of soldiers in tanks, and the political artists retreat into chemical cages instead of being thrown into real ones.

I've spent a lot of time feeling furious with language, with my own inability to talk about what's going on, with the weakness of our movements and of the forms that dominate political expression. I've been trying to get away from the idea that I need to sum it up in the way that I just did. I've been thinking of poems as more like paintings, sketches, snapshots, unexpected angles of perception. I need to go quicker, trust to chance more, stop labouring over things in an attempt to see all the connections or to represent them accurately. Too much of our culture is focused on people trying to explain themselves, to say where they've come from, what they mean, who they are, etc. I would rather all of those things remain fundamentally obscure. Why should I feel more proximity to an artist making work about austerity in the South East of England than e.g. a poet dying in a prison hospital in Tehran? Which life do I want to lead? What is the radius of the solidarity that I am capable of feeling or projecting?

Here's another thought. Earlier this year a theatre-maker who was important to me once killed himself after he was arrested for possession of child pornography and I started to see all of his art and writing as a kind of addiction, a lifelong, hundreds-of-thousands-of-words-long circumlocution, an endless failure to get to the fucking point, to just come out and say it, to admit what was happening with him, and I started to think about other people I have known who have been addicted, you for example, but also friends of mine who have died, my cousin who just got out of hospital where he was sectioned after a drug induced psychosis, my own compulsive behaviours. I thought about the students my mum used to work with in her FE college who would constantly self-harm because they got so angry about their inability to complete the maths and

English tests they had to pass in order to get their builders' NVQ or whatever. Self-harm and art-making have always been bound up for me, implicitly and explicitly. Partly as opposites – compulsive self-harm arises from a failure of language, from the inability to speak, from mute frustration at the unwieldiness or paucity of our thinking – but also as twins, or as different forms of the same reality. It feels obvious now that I write it. Of course just because you have enough language to say something about who you are or how you perceive reality it doesn't mean you have enough to say what it is that you need to say, or to say the right thing. Just because you've received enough education to write a fucking poem or a play instead of punching a wall or cutting yourself, it doesn't mean the frustration magically disappears – that the expression is true, that the language is correct, that the artwork expresses or communicates what it needs to. Most of the time it doesn't. Frustration is just lifted up onto a new plane, and the harms that are implicit to that state are transmuted. For a long time this year I wanted to be fucking illiterate. I tried to write poems about what was going on in my life and the political world that feels so far away and I just felt defeated. I felt sick with my language and wanted to get out of it, into muteness or oblivion, and I tried in my mind or sitting in front of a computer screen to punch my way out of it, to create inside of language a version of that wall that we punch when we want to find a way into it but can't and end up communicating crudely with our bodies instead; and I see now really for the first time that in the end there is just one wall, with people beating with their fists on it from both sides, and always stupidly imagining that it's a building with internal volume and not just a flat two-dimensional space. There's been times in my life when I have been more aware of this pattern and more determined to find a way out of it, and there have been times when I've felt a kind of perverse pride in it and have thought of it like a 'fuck you' to all of my better and more privileged instincts: but it's always there, inside of me, along with all of the people in my life who have succumbed to their addictions, or who live with them, like you and Sean and my paranoid cousin and Chris whose paedophilia consumed him.

Some other things I wrote down in my phone while I was sitting in hospitals: "Poetry is inhibited by the desire for knowledge. The desire for knowledge is insatiable. It tells you you're not ready to begin yet. But that's not right. When you sit in a hospital and listen to people talking on the phone about the cancer surging through their bodies you know there is no time to wait, and that poetry is the only thing there is." "I walked with my severed head to the church." "These experiment Pictures have been bruized and knocked about, without mercy, to try all experiments."

I didn't have a resolution at New Years, so maybe I can have some now. I resolve to drastically lower the bar for expression. All my most instinctive sympathies are with people who don't know how to talk anyway, and especially the ones who get defensive and lash out and say the worst things possible. Why should I reproduce in art all of the same impossible standards that I oppose in everyday politics? I think that William Blake was right when he said that if you can't achieve an effect you want QUICKLY then it will probably do more damage than it's worth, and that it only exists anyway because some ruling class artists have other people to do their technical work for them. I love the design you made for the cover of *I/II* because it preempted that realisation by introducing into the poem all these BREAKS and abrasive non-continuities, at a time when in my own mind it was still a sort of solid unbroken surface – basically a kind of wall, which I could get up and start punching every day without really knowing why it was that I was doing it, or where the need was coming from.

I could try to finish this with some elegant analogy between art and class politics or artistic form and society, but that's not really what I'm aiming for here. Lucidity is just a wall; you can throw yourself against it from either side but it has no internal dimensions; we need to keep moving. Like you said,

"Every step is still on the march. sometimes we are together sitting thats sitting on the march thats eating on the march going to the cinema restaurant on the march new garms on the march on the march doing the crimes doing drugs bickering on The march, we split apart re congregate but we are always marching it doesn't stop. Its a whole other domain its here as well."

Its here as well. That's something I have to keep reminding myself.

Solidarity,
Danny

Loading Terminal

Before that. Beneath the first arch. I'm always climbing back up out of myself, out of the drama or school-run bus stop of my own unresponsiveness. Loving someone who has 'advanced' cancer demands that you shut off the future in a kind of instinctive solidarity. We are here now. The portal we need to pass through leads into this present. There are so many things that prevent us from going through it. 'Speed', writes Celan, 'which has always been "outside", has gained yet more speed. The poem knows this but heads straight for the "otherness" which it considers it can reach and be free, which is perhaps vacant'. 'Speed has gained yet more speed'. 'The poem knows this'. In Kafka the walkthrough metal detectors (he called them 'laws') always lead to more metal detectors with bigger gatekeepers, a word which right now has quite a lot of currency on the London activist scene in which I live, though many of the gatekeepers here in this world are Black and Asian council workers who know better than Kafka's *Turhüter* the difficulties of 'passing through'.

"Not until we reach the extreme confines of life, in the arctic regions or on the borders of an utter desert, will competition cease."

It turns out it's not so easy to combine this reality and your everyday life, rhythms, and mental worlds. In the history of poetry and of mythology-religion the gate is the site of the test or trial, the place where invisible moral powers and capacities are finally assayed and confirmed or found wanting. In Kafka it was cleverly rotated 90 degrees until it resembled a trench: fuck the idea of ennoblement through trial or test of endurance, its vision of redemption through violence and all the hierarchies that are based on it. Go into a Jamaican restaurant in Hackney, look at the pictures of the celebrated sprinters on the wall: A people who have been denied access to the moral test and so who have learned to excel through speed that gained more speed probably isn't what Paul Celan had in mind, but here it is. Today the gate is a place where people are denied access to resources by people who resemble them: conflict ceases to be 'structural' and 'predictable' and becomes personal, volatile, and impossible to second guess, and so also unconscionable from the perspective of a political liberalism that is always up for a struggle so long as it passes the impossible trial of purity that that same liberalism inevitably poses to it – the gate that has gained more gate. I want poetry to deal not just with the great stirring conflicts of 'our society' but with competition at its utter borders and in its arctic regions as well. Gatekeeper conflicts. Personal antagonisms. That's *my* highway of despair, and if it too leads only into the present then it leads further into it, the presence has gained more presence, the speed that has gained more speed has gained more speed still, and we know this but head straight for the otherness where we consider we can be more free.

0 - To my greeder

More nights than I know how to speak of. Crushed stone, sand and gravel.
A bleeding body lying next to its travel bag, still upright.
The rapid expansion of airports, or a ringroad, surrounding an unbuilt city.
A language that can be called revolutionary, or pointless, depending on
perspective.
Secretly I read your work every night

* *

Larissa Reisner, I'm standing at my balcony window.
Pulling back the Untitled steel and steel mesh curtains,
the nails on my left hand are painted blue.
I see a city you left behind

in the year twenty twenty two, long since abandoned

**

I can't help it

Blue flowers,
black champagne. Objects without interiors
Wars. Cenesis.
The poetry of Nora Colleen Fulton
a steel parachute unfolding
like a sequin
in the sodium light of a streetlamp.

I wrote about bigots and conspiracy theorists
because people who are driven
to thoughts
for reasons other than their respectability
have my sympathy,
even when the thoughts themselves are clearly false
or exaggerate a prejudice

already preached to us
in chastely
homeopathic doses.

Almost by definition
those who do the greatest harm
will think things
that are essentially
inoffensive:
A creature that lives for only 24 hours
has no evolutionary use
for a mouth

**

An interstate highway system.
Last night, in a metal bed, followed by a general decline for the next thirty years.

In fact the freedom that has been promoted has always been economic.

The OECD takes an interest in 'all the phases of organized matter'

As I watch you dress, the way your bones have changed makes me think of

(light crudes, steel and steel mesh, red and white high tension. Concrete.)

Methane. March dusk.

1

loading terminal. the prison trains leave the ghost stations by night in critically melting

shadow the tunnels, granulated like emerald potash bend and steel, the British disease

deniers rush out into the Streets to wave their impetuous hankies. it is not time

to speak of the sanitary greenhouses and the sea's ceaseless mutations it is still, here

the 400 hectare greenhouse will coast above the seas' atypical pseudohorizons
as

thru veils of steel tears we watch as a hundred crush barriers crumble. it is time

The New Great Market of Bodies is created where the antipsychotics wear off,
in snows

of precious stones the white coated staff are bored and a red scare podcast falls
softly

like snowflakes through thousands of surfaces to the surface of solid gold lake

it is hip and cynically affectless on the vast iron roof we first felt it in thousand
s

of those tiny red bits we did not read the news, or know the names of the politi
cal groups.

we didnt know who's at war with who. we couldn't care less about the scandal

Nights I would look out through the vast glass walls of the greenhouse a massi
ve

emptiness would provide atmosphere the trains would pass in melting emerald
sheets:

I wear my windrunner with a adidas gasmask. a thin rain scans me, I am weak.

One day a lump appeared in my body I put on my Hugo poly crew & went out
into an inbred sea

behind me the days on this earth appeared dead like Seas but I did not think of
them

my mind was empty of everything but what I need: these Gas-masks stink of it

Don't think. Certain images drew me on the vast iron wall its distances measur
ed by metal detectors

we walk through certain regions of this wish not to be like them and the feeling
that

I'd rather die than be just another educated liberal and all the damage that that

feeling can cause to others as well as ourselves and all its distances, measured by
metal

detectors we walk through to the vast iron wall where nothing is as it seems &

an inbred

ocean, trembling, branches out in roots fibrous & stateless: a thin rain scans it.

I put on my BOSS swim shorts and went out the 20p toilets hung there on four
silk-thin

strings things I cannot say tremble inside of them they are like shit up its Wall
the 20p

coins in my pocket vibrate, the shit is cleaned, but still our gas masks stink of it.

Certain images draw me on an image of what cleans an image of what pollutes
an image

of what blocks and of what communicates I stood in the corroding thin rain, a
image of

myself flickering in the particle 'of', in greenhouses of negation: pseudoradical

One day a lump appeared in my body, I put on some clothes made by slaves &
went out

there for nothing in particular. I was soaked by the sea it was inbred by entrepr
eneurs

to enhance its wetness its vastness and in particular its character as a boundary

in the middle of that sea I met the image of myself it askd me how is it that we are able

to see the hatred of appearance wrap itself in reality when in reality all we ever wanted

was to appear, and why have we concealed that reality behind this vast iron wall

searching for a tiny red bit of negation in vast greenhouses of nihilism why is it that

Our Originals boyfriend hoodie is torn when all things are changed, even as in ancient times.

where 1000s of these rivers in veins Of blood pour silently down the mountains

the image sweeps past me in tears of allegoric rage, & in boredom I sweep past it it

travels toward meaning but I travel towards meaning-death you may think this is

white middle class shit but try actually writing a poem while wearing a gasmask.

one day you 2 will throw up the small emotional palette in a tiny very expensive
sushi restaurant

looking out the window you will see the 20p toilet turn on four perfect silkthin
strings:

matchsticks & dice float on the surface of a lake, & a 1000 surfaces rise from it

Up the Lorazepam. A voice will say to you, 'the truth is there. you write whats
said

and you don't lie. demented I rushed madly up and down & hurled myself into
traffic,

bang my head with all my force against the walls. nothing changes: red dice &

matchsticks are still falling, even now; the rich people won't survive Hackney
a lake not of Waters but of Space'

and deep inside this hip hatred of appearances Fumiko Kaneko stands trial, &
at her silent

endlessly repeated insistence new verbs are adapted to new conditions of hunger

These feelings can cause others to dance as well as ourselves, & through all its
distances measured by metal
detectors we walk through alarmed phrases to a cast Iron hall where nothing is
& write down our slogan:
it is as it seems. & this blend of advertising & politics brings us right back now

to where the breeding of the ocean first started. I know, I know I'm getting ahead
of myself;
the road stretches out before us through tinted one-way languages & dead trees
washed up in
the deep brain, like grey foam at the edge of a river, all my gasmasks stink of it

for whatever counts as time, Whatever you do, don't think. the official podcast
plays on repeat
& in the 1000th reinforced greenhouse the die and the matchsticks have fallen.
turn around
pull your foreskin back, get dressed. This is a venereal war between high rises:

the working class has no official Opinion. In the greenhouse official blue birds settle on

our official shoulders & sing their official melody, as along the shore of every
ocean

a star rises above muscular waters, lighting the vast iron wall & the 20p toilet.

shove your Heaven. March 8, 9.30 in the morning, everything that I remember
drifts in Eternity's states

of pure compression. I look out the wall of the greenhouse, at the massive split
glass

sheets now due to be replaced with new types of carbonfibre reinforced plastic

despite it, certain images draw me on. one day this lump appeared in my body,
I put on my Airmax Genomes and go out:

did the inbred seas stir in that greenhouse, did the official podcast play a decibel
louder?

silent I looked out upon a 1000 walkthru security gates & a thin rain scanned me

II – Focus Group

And behind barbed wire
In the dense heart of the warehouse
My double is sent for interrogation
With two thugs sent by the noseless dick
And I hear the sound of my own voice:

Airlift me out

shove your art
you think they celebrate you, in a cemetery of peaches, in a big cage
for a change the maroon wetlands
shifts
aims to be ugly, scenes like all they wanted is memory I dare you

now suicidewatch at Wormwood Scrubs begins, beneath the massive grey elevations

the giant empty ships, all that soppy shit

our wetsuits

aroused torchlight, in the poppy red rain it is I have nothing

smells of sweat, mingling, above the seas of black lilies

do you think they give a shit about a rink in a vast greenhouse

don't think.

You give them what they need, that's all

today aldi is the biggest company in the world, but it is lit by a single ring

washed out red, wedding torchlight, inside an abstract & impersonal they

will you lower me please

Blue rinks one after the other twist in memory, I see hulls as wide as

thin

planets move in ellipses, fluorescent, phosphorescent, gay estranged

realities seem to fuse in this core, dovelike, and pierce the future,

fuck you

ignorant lower welded hulls inside an stereotypical company executive
pours like shadows from a highstreet Ladbrokes
staggering

guiltless into the rink's dark crowds, they dont need you think
here they are just hints of
he pauses, as rinks fall silently from memory, in tenuous ancestral
arcs
of hesitant blue, like shadows from a highstreet Ladbrokes

my cousin's meth habit
twisted beneath a massive heightened street of air an empty pipeline you
sellout millimetres
of abattoir beneath these, miles of nightclubs it all disappear as it really is
guiltless

Red carpet, golden cousin,
come quick
shove your physical limitations I imitate this millionth greenhouse

a few millimetres away in its vomit strewn party district
nighttime streetsweepers

begin beneath a maze of imitations of, juxtapose distance with
he pause, the metal has already dazeddigital,
the elevator falled from memory
one after the other,
to warn the blunt rink, without a word about what working class art really 'is'

Shove your conservative and identitarian insistence this is
our art, cool to the point of being able
to touch it without burning
on the empty giant ships or in the large cellular vans,
did you think they would just need you, the giant iron ore mines are just mms

away we control all relations, there are no physical limits.
fuck getting in the car, enjoying world class services
they don't want
your 'poetical inventions'

your vast 'greenhouse' and no they don't want your biography either.

now watch the giant distances grow inside the vast cellular vehicles. it is
millimetre-
thick glass concealing new depths and dimensions. a simple trick,
to touch it without burning
the greenhouse and the whole sky and fucking everything I said before

all literature
tries to masturbate in an empty Leeds hotel room; so what if they
reverse nightfall, pretending what is and will be
At COP26,
the seventy GMB stewards assigned to protect Greta Thunberg are sacrificed

to the now rearranged crowd, which pours from night's SUV is not celibate
blue light in the toilet so what if they did,
try to understand
who you are pigs, the eternal footpath is carved in deep letters on the
innumerable, willowing sands

nighttime suicidewatch begins, in the empty black metal detectors

Dalston is owned by pigs, and a miraculous blue mirage glides smoothly

from the rink's five surfaces

beneath the emblematic blank metal detectors' 1,000 acre reinforced glass,

felicitous

low SUV curtain flutter in the nights, scrub nightshift begins all over

the greenhouse

electric lights sweep lyrically through those sketchy, enigmatical bars,

an era

begins on all fours, a nightshift, everywhere the same infinity of lesser

worlds wanks off the greater you can hear this weak smattering of

applause:

you can be the hottest brand in the world, blue mineral five figure senses

street methamphetamine coming out your eyes like Rilke, Mallarmé,

Vida Brest,

all these manganese alloys, below the low manganese smashed

up northern towns

erupt pound something away, you can have it all down to a 't', blue

billboards

with your face on stretch away, like fingernails beneath the massive grey

(the grow-lights

Already spoken for empty louis vuitton lifeboats glisten and low,

Vast tear gas canisters, feel the distance

skylines

tremor & palsied, with a bleak visual effects you can get away not saying

anything about your life, the law the lives of the people around you, sprints

in the canisters the theatre the thousands of levels of morphine you're

reminded

by each

difference falls, on that glass and runs on hedonists, scratch another

100 nights of this blue, I'm tired of this too visceral effect, begins

a hundred acres away nightshifts, the hull stretch like fingernails beneath us
and the billboards are like dots. Come now,
tremor for the weak and vile metal detectors, out on his 'escorted walk' is he
my cousin

gets off at some emotions, square easily the following night acres
through the canisters flames, stay
here, you are the treatment, poor or disabled in a theatre, with 1000s of levels it is a
complete work of art,
bailiffs from some unremembered world now you can repeat it

Shove your art. shove all those manganese alloys, they are merely flashes
double in a meters, gas Friday nights you can spill out your guts right
now you can inch through the canisters' flames
same
distance already you can be the tissues of everybody's lips, in 8 events across

five cities, a weak smattering of applause, a nightshift. In the 20p toilets
a new era begins with

new words you don't know burning houses and all their perfect circular arcs.

shove your art,

just another in the series sprint down the stairs

a nightshift, thudding through the metal detector a complete redefinition

of all interiors

all these words you don't know whipped across the rink with the force of an

abyss.

Shove that literalism, we wont swallow their vomit or grey wine

'all great things perish by their own accord, by a deliberate act of creation'

that's not us.

I'm common and my talking's quite abrupt

uppers

release repressive collectivity, utter garbage of sensation, speak of endless

utter gardens, vehicle showrooms, mosques. all my friends think they're being

watched.

you can play around with stereotypes all you want. metal detectors in the

skies

vast oval, billions of senses, a nightshift beneath the elevators' vast corridors:

etc.

*
*

Dear danny, everything I make I want to fuck it up,
            no one eats the illiterate bake
seabulk by the black wind, earning millions for that reap
clearly the idiots
replies you didn't heal them, not with this alcoholic
            wreck
I see and sun and clouds, shitty and kitsch pattern confess
            Guardianista

I didn't want, impression. life moves
you ride through everything I do, the rain
the ordinary meeting, everything
            The main arterial routes fuck and shit money like rain,
shrinking like Honeywell and BASF and Shell.
That is my anarchism clearly, hated Sheraton
forest death in a vast meaningless engine of thought
keep it simple.

III – Hospitals

The New Great Market of Bodies is created where the antipsychotics wear off:
we are

immune to precious stones as I write this my comrades are deported, and their
vehicles

impounded. We are one step closer to new verbs for new conditions of hunger

then I showered and got dressed. march whatever, some hour, some minute in
forever

In London its essence is sold in pill form on the internet I admit
this

beneath some blank impersonal skies, some banged city of mopeds. shove

an era beneath an empty rose coloured sky, pale opalescent stars move
back and for

a moment we are all there is blue figurines, come quick your shift banged

millimetres
at my side, stale language I don't need beneath the elevator got through by

now this and what's the point of crying. I remember, the same shit. pale blue
music
beneath an empty roadworks begin again the moment a red light crosses
through the bonfire
spreads, motionless beneath us like a emerald tree rashes out removed loans

empathy, like emeralds on the pavements far below. don't judge, but give us
knowledge of the vast iron wall
of our state, take its law into our hands, wank off as many worlds as I
can make
model languages, of another language outside of this one, ticking like a

limit to creation slaps, shove your Heaven. March 8, 9.30 in the morning
everything I remember drifts in Eternity's
state of
pure compression

sleeps in parked cars are you cracked, distinct emotional effects are you

break someone sitting there, like an emerald on the pavements far below.
listen.
assonances of a trace language. music videos are a totally distinct and inferior
kind of poetry,
like the wank racist unions which hinder the vision of god. those who

spend their lives crumbling in blue houses rows of parked cars filled with
concrete
forests and forms the colours of pork gone off, you think they don't know,
you think
you cruise through them ruined and recreated by dead snows

by some kind of force, like density and lightness, continua and sudden steam
break shifts damn
fucker you don't low levels of excitation collide loosely
in my chest
pitcher of Taittinger Comtes de Champagne, KA sparkling black grape

stain the night air I envy their balloons and stunted rose gardens, cunts
of Frieze
'I cannot' scorched into my retinas, like emeralds on the pavement outside are
you cast out
from Heaven every junkie knows you are not, well crust of fried flesh

everybody can be an intelligent, famed for attractively formed opinions
as my mingled taste
crashes emeralds scatter on a wave I do not know your sushi restaurants
or dyed
heretical eyelids of the sun I do not see that Orcus of What Has Been

but teach the grapes inside my mind to wink, which is a fire to me as we have
groped
for valves, sexualised massage, and I will give off lights that do not sweat
but vapes
new drainage systems, generous funding fuck all we have grown up

among the embers; the granite care home wanks inside our head like a dog
we have
eaten from the alien art warehouse. and in the cold zones of molecular clouds
I know
'I cannot see' is scorched into my retinas, like rubies in the phone box outside

can scatter in the toilets deny this emeralds in the remote witness evidence
room scored out
come quick, Dior ultracycle, dead dream, dead trans artist I mourn the fuck
out of this art we are all approaching emphases
every junkie knows,

others I scarcely see simply slipped over the nose and pulled into position.
to represent each rim
of scum beneath the sea, bruised and knocked about like a idiot injunctio
banish
that speech it isnt ideas that define reality it doesn't matter whose heads theyre in

Existing by perception and by fire I can no longer accept, strips of very rich

people, grief swastikas
arousal I mean really smash their heads against the pavement and then say
they
were resisting arrest. pornographical or didactic ripe serene tube strike eclair,

drastically lower the bar to snapshot random hollowness. In my thoughts,
it felt like
any of us could set London alight for six months, hate speech filed through
our thoughts like
emeralds, filled with gas pipes and water, spineless, cringing and crawling.

dawns glisten. I won't stop writing 'poetry' yet just to beg a 'audience'.
as Ideas are not
the reality of a person any more than wallpaper is the reality of a skyscraper
or the sudden opening
& closing of a prison's interior doors afford any suggestion of freedom

we are as we perceive, and even if our own Ideas strip like a screw on the line
strips,

it will merely alleviate the monotony.
dawn glistens
The greenhouse's beautiful lights fall

on beautiful people. excruciate their rights. Shove your art. March 11, 6.30
in the morning
I console myself for having lost Jerusalem. the grey world outside barely
shifts
seas piled on top of seas, thiamethoxam green apples fallen slowly from the

roofs. Am I right. this morning it rains and then brightens. almost all these
ambulance drivers
are West African or Caribbean. we talk in the common areas
as they
maneouvre your wheelchair toward the lifts. 'stay strong. god bless'.

today I am afraid of being just another educated liberal it fucking eats me
from
the inside like a vast underground lake. through the windows the umbilical

cords
search for something vile anything to say

centuries rain symbols of authority on the pornographic landscape of a
Clyde
Alpha Jerusalem, Audis parked up outside the estates. you can't explain it
but it
fucks your head up anyway, every day

pulsing through you
like a smashed emerald on the pavement, far below the desire to make
all our
lives better
the wish not to be like them, like waves across the phantom sea

separates and spreads out towards the shore, far below 'benevolence'
split
scree of semi-coherence and all the bullshit about justice the wish not to be
like them

in Depth of Form and vile pulsing membranes without Colour It is only this

wish which moves me through what Vileness I create I see An outer rings
radiance

pass from it like shadows of an emerald It is the essence of everything I do
giving it

depth and substance everything else is shrill vile unbelievable casual

sex fascist Decollated and hung like souls where did it come from, these basic
words

Colour everything we say glisten anyway Every Day we walk past it,
the strategically

placed crush barrier in full view of the sanitary Greenhouse from the sea

small rivers flow into small regions of the brain, and through it an immense
temporary world's

first halting words a new language I couldn't care less about masturbate
in a phone

box no empire sect or star can create the things you love like an iron wall

or smash reality as a whole. it just isn't that simple. These states exist,
& throughout them all
I see the tunnel in my mind a 1,000 metal detectors away
it hangs
above a phantom sea in skies of curves and infinite series it represents stages

which have already been completed which my mind passes through like waves
across a phantom sea:
everything which Exists passes through a thousand metal detectors unafraid of
educated liberalism
or any of these other dormant sheets of melody, the smell of weed smoke on

the stairs of shit and blood in public toilets cannot deceive them Nor can
exquisite
words pass through them all carefully chosen language ostentatious vile casual
sex
scandal decollated and slurs are as visible to them as bedding in a phone box is

where thousands of rivers in veins Of blood pour down the mountains they are
assimilated, they are not felt.
you asked me if there was a lump and I said no a vast iron wall thousands of
metal detectors
I don't remember these Images they come back now in place of my life An

oncologist sweeps past us she ceases to Exist but the people cycling food
through
the night never do they are like waves on a phantom sea they only Exist by
passing.
shove your elite anaesthetic

production culture we want the other, the unconditional, the new vast tunnel in
my mind
a bright flash
a 1,000
acre greenhouse seen through the windows of an armoured car above terraced

houses the fear of being like them rising like a bright new moon. it hangs

above the
plantation seas
in skies of magnetic glass cement:
is it too soon?

An oncologist sweeps past us. March 0th
the desolate
hatred I then felt was a kind of liberation, because it was ugly hatred,
conscious
Ugly hatred created in my Mind not as a position which can only be born

but as a state, which burns up as soon as I look away it will not be regenerated.
Euphoric
Reduce me to
nothing
remix: Wild swans' filth on a vast metal surface, images of a tower,

of the sun rising through mist in a frozen garden like a tiny red balloon now it
floats

in my artery: 'they will punish you for any attempt to get off the sick & they will

torture you for being on it'. like waste which accumulates in our cells like shit

in a toilet like this feeling of something always bubbling beneath the surface of an

image that spreads out in every conceivable direction, these states Exist to extend and the Swans in rapture beat

their brilliant wings against the brilliant portals: no more irons,

no more mourning, no more
false alarms.
We pass through deforested iron roofs like cannon fodder. We laugh at those
persons who cannot connect the electric gates at the end of a country drive,
the cancer

in their bodies and the cancelled parts of speech. no more michel houellebecq
no more boredom
no more

hurt,
Cecilia Vicuña says you know a poem's too long when your ass gets tired,

Come out of the toilets and wipe your hands on your shirt. the solar boats will travel
through such gates. we're all the gods of transitions times doorways passages & endings.
Don't make us puke we said I'm not afraid of being like them. 'Although one

stated meaning can be determined in so many different ways', some people flatter
themselves there will be No Last Judgment & that bad art will be adopted & Mixed
with good yet they deceive themselves their Positions burn up the moment

we cease to behold them then Ugliness and Beauty will appear 'What' it will be questioned
'When the Sun rises do you not see a round Disk of red somewhat like a balloon?

O no no I say I see an innumerable company of

the Heavenly host crying bullshit bullshit bullshit the collapse of the tunnel in
my mind
is no catastrophe I question not the Rage I have felt any more than I would
question
anyone who fights lashing out I lash out with and against them END

**

Originals boyfriend hoodie stained with breast milk, come quick
the gates are all rotten,
A threshold burns and goes out.
there are no more assumptions, no waste of freedom.
only fingers on assholes in beds made from lice. the colourless stamen
climbing upwards through the alien structures, Black beads for eyes

Don't think. There are no stars: dis-astra.
The Voicenotes have all gone blue with distortion, Ghanaian drums.
'The proud tradition of all who stood up and said no' can fuck itself.
I walked down that tunnel
I know Airmax Genomes give you cancer. Here I am,

it is the gates and the limitations themselves that are dead,
I don't need a boundary to sustain me. I don't fuck with that absence.
Let the dead people speak at the rally, 3.6 Fahrenheit.
'When you do it, it becomes possible'
I have lived w/out light and electricity. I have walked down that tunnel. here I am.

IV – A thousand years later

We speak the new dialect now. Trains ride silently through the cancer wards
by night
the destroyed armoured vehicles weep in the emerald shadow of the meat mark
ets

where the antigens all wore off, tiny flowing evolving flowers that never cease

I cant keep them and so I throw up my hands and they fly out over the rampart
s

virtue signalling silently tore through the freight ships and four-lane motorway
s

the materials research labs and Science parks and Business parks all gone now

in the new film by Benny and Josh there is a perfect replica of Time and Space
we cried when we saw it
in the great market the greenhouse cried and evolved a winter garden from tiny

red bits
above us the bloody pink tracksuit of the sky cried, & thick fires contend w rain

Of the poem 'u ride through everything I make, the rain, the ordinary meeting'
there's really
not much more to say: the main arterial road fucks and shits money like rainx
blown
on a emerald wind, & the shadows cast by the greenhouse lengthen our nights

as a New Era begins on all fours. The lump we had found then spread rapidly
undetected
through a 1000 metal detectors, its fine silk strings turn in the dusk's emerald
winds
drunks stagger on the gold surface of their antipsychotics they see, they do not

of the poem 'originals boyfriend hoodie stained with breast milk. come quick'
only
a tonne of pig aluminium remains, rained upon in a loading terminal it cannot
move us,

We know that there was something there even though we can no longer see it,

spreading down my spine & in my breast like a simple silk string. Of the poem
'shove your art'

the wind and the thick fires contend with it, antipsychotic gold lumps grow on
it, it

vibrates, and the metal detectors all buckle beneath stained with breast milk skies

We watch as people disembark from the train they rush through a 1000 prisons
to the

Future anterior and look back at the Metal Detectors they have passed through
them

but their trauma has not it is detained by those gates as the unfossilizable parts

of organisms that are remembered by amber thus they can judge of themselves
that which is

eternal & that which annihilable, the limited structural capacities of our move
ments are

overcome the lump spreads like new wings, & the thick fires contend with rain

In the new film by Benny and Josh there is a perfect replica of Time and Space
we cried when we saw it
in the great market the greenhouse cryd and evolves a summer garden in tiny red
bits

above us the bloody pink tracksuit of the sky cried, & thick fires contend w rain

but they were tears of joy not of anger or of rage the last episode of the podcast
red scare
has filled this time and space exhausting it 1,000 x over as we watched from the
summer garden
We knew that it would remember everything, even what I am thinking now that

there is a poetry corresponding to every mental state, every circumstance, every
amount
of available energy. Only certain forms can be taken from us, not poetry itself,
since poetry
is the registration of what has been taken and so gains from what we lose, even

the strongest and deepest-thinking poet can only write strong and deep-thinking poems,

but there are a thousand other kinds! Even a thousand of them is nothing to be proud about.

& we look back across the metal detectors we are no longer afraid of becoming

Of the poem 'this is our art', not much is left; only these amber and white dots still fall

on the surface of the lake reminding us of the giant empty ship that once moved there thru

1,000s of Gold Surfaces in corroding fire, we are no longer afraid of becoming

we are no longer afraid of becoming, this thought passes through us like the shadow of an emerald

it radiates from the essence of everything like the wish not to be like them it is itself

essenceless and the two thoughts struggle in the night like thick fire and rainx

& this is our art, cool to the point of being able to touch it without burning on

the giant
empty ships or in the large Cellular vans. did you really think they didnt need
it?
secretly they read it every night, their giant iron mines spread out around them

in the great market of bodies no more of them will be coming & in the peeling
platinum
suburbs of greenhouses the helicopterferries soil the night, it is as if the new film
by benny
never happend that pitiful shit is washed off, and new rain falls, but a fire was

Of the vast iron wall – well, that's where we are right now, a vice documentary
crew
captured everything as it happend we passd through the final security gate into
the new
elevators the last shipment of emeralds departs & lovers in the audience weep

tears into the inbred sea it rises in Fury and trembling overflowing the Market
of

Bodies its phantom waves pave it leaving this flat Fe surface over which today we walk

crying tears of joy not of rage we come & go as we please no rain will scan us

We put on our Nike jacket and went up, the cameras linger on us last rains run away

in calm gentle errorprone streams towards the lake's golden and antipsychotic surface,

it is as it seems we kneel & trace the slogan i am no longer afraid of becoming

as for the cunts whose food is carried to them up a 1,000 stairs, I guess its true they

don't Exist now, but the wish not to be like them isn't something I can really feel anymore

it's like something in us has been set free: the rainx fall, but the fire will not be.

Loading terminal. The prison trains reach their ghost destination and the Pigs all disembark

now they look around themselves in curiosity at many tonnes of stord pig iron

aluminium
podcasts play over the intercom but they dont hear them. I now lay down the pen

with which I have written this clumsy account, my presence will soon be effaced
from
this earth. I believe that every real phenomenon continues as such to exist even
though
it be obliterated in eternal actuality. there is now poetry corresponding to every

circumstance, every physical state, every degree of energy, to every new species
of sea;
the wars between the high rises have ceased without producing even a single
golden slogan
& as for me, well. there was a time in my life when I was so afraid of beautiful

moral appearances that I couldnt tear my eyes off the greenhouse and the cunts
of
frieze who work in my mind wept their steel tears beneath a metal detector arch
but not now.

I'm not afraid of becoming anything now, even this. even a wish not to be like

them shifts beneath these shitty allegories like bones changing beneath surface

s

of our skin. so the antigens wear off in snows of precious stones but what now

so

virtue signalling silently tore through the freight ships and four-lane motorways

but what now? is there nothing to hate but the appearance-preventer? not even.
later,

behind this vast iron wall, a tiny red bit of negation in a vast greenhouse of nih

appears.

it is about a 1000 metal detectors away, we see it slowly filling the greenhouse.

with its light a new day begins new poetries begin to be written but shove their

now

it grows brighter and ever increasingly brighter & we race down from the wall

toward

the loading terminal where the trains all depart. Intel warfare. back to the start.

Acknowledgements

Climate and Resilience was originally published in May 2021 on 87 Press's online platform The Hythe. *I/II* was published by Shit Valley in 2017. Two of the poems in the section 'High Volume Bulk' were published in *Erotoplasty* in 2019; a third came out in *VOLUME (for JHP)* in 2021. The letter to Sophie Carapetian was written for *Refuse to Collaborate* (Stadtgalerie Bern, 2022). *Advice Column* and *At Close Range* first washed up on Free Trials (www.pxxtry.com) in 2019 and 2021, respectively, and the poem 'Loading Terminal' was piped in from the Caspian Basin in the first months of 2022. Ines Doujak very kindly allowed me to use a piece from her *Geistervölker* series for the cover, Will Holder rescued me from some typographical problems, Luke Roberts from some chronological ones, and Dom Hale supplied some words for the blurb. My thanks to all the infrastructure builders.

UNDER THE WORLD

NIGHT OF THE WORLD 2

By Oscar Guardiola-Rivera

Published 2024 by the87press

The 87 Press LTD

87 Stonecot Hill

Sutton

Surrey

SM3 9HJ

www.the87press.co.uk

Under the World: Night of the World 2

ISBN: 978-1-7393939-7-7

Printed and bound by CPI Group (UK) Ltd, Croydon, CR0 4YY

Cover image: #bajas IV by Greta Chicheri (2013) with the author's permission.

Design: Stanislava Stoilova [www.sdesign.graphics]

Inspired by the Mayan Book of the Dawn of Life,
Popol Vuh

Contents

Prologue

This manuscript may be read
as a roots rave manifesto
to free literature,
its wider space
its dark matter,
of memory and theatre.

An invitation
to make a sideways move,
dance and turn
to re-turn
from the absolute reign of
linear composition
in novels and linear narratives,
to the plebeian
texts
of image, object, and sound
that can be found
throughout the native Americas.

The tree, the trunk, and the roots,
the past-future,
to which we're bound.

Looking forwards,
to futures past,
we move backwards.

To envision an inhabitable future,
perhaps we would do well
to find a rock crevice,

an entry
into the underground,
and go backward.

To find our roots,
perhaps we would do well
looking for them where roots are usually found.

It is as she says,
the seer of this tale:

"At least the Spirit of Place
is a more benign one
than the exclusive
and aggressive
Spirit of Race."[1]

This is an invitation provocation.

To call for a revolution
in the kingdom of plot,
which is no longer a lighthouse,
but a wreckers' lantern
luring us aground

in the **night of the world**

to loot us.

This is also a tale,

---

[1] Ursula K. Le Guin, "A Non-Euclidean View of California as a Cold Place to Be," in Thomas More's *Utopia*, intr. by China Miéville with essays by U. K. Le Guin (London: Verso, 2016) 171-2.

or the discontinuity of a tale
told in the old form of a katabasis.
About what happened to Hoodoo Girl
after she fought an inquisitor witch
at sea
and trapped hope,
a trickster named Ix,
who may or may not be her sister and lover,
to see
the new day
in the bottom of a jar.

Where is she/they?

Like the rest of us.
In the dark.

Episode 1. In the Dark

I Am ~~Not~~ Here

I am ~~not~~ here.
I could ~~not~~ be.
Do ~~not~~ ask my name.

For I lost it the same night
I lost
my crew
my friends
my mirror and soul.
The same night
I turned,
or returned,
backwards in time.
Do not ask for my story.
It isn't as if I have forgotten who I am
or what my story is.
(Perhaps I have)
More truthful it would be
for you to figure
(out/down & out)
what is like
to be conscripted into
History
as I was.
By negation,
Backwards,
upside down,
and falling downwards.
Disinherited from a past
that was never properly ours,
displaced
violated

from behind.
Damned,
Condemned
to be out of place
brought to a phantom place
where history never took place
As it should.
My story is a bad story.
A wayward story.
It organised
my family story,
our inner lives.
"This waywardness
Organized our inner lives."[2]
It's the same with all of us,
the people of Caliban.
We were displaced,
brought from somewhere else into this
nowhere place,
without beginning or a tall tale of origins
to call our own,
dispossessed of a history
that was never ours in the first place.
So, do ~~not~~ ask what happened to me.
I've told you already.
I was at sea. Unable to see
for I had lost my mirror and soul.
That is why now
I have no precise way
of collecting in a tight line & plot
the chain of causes or agency

---

[2] Stuart Hall with Bill Schwarz, *Familiar Stranger. A Life Between Two Islands* (London: Penguin, 2017) 61.

that brought me here.
I have
No pedantic way.
No precise way.
No linear method
to bring the pieces together
in a manner that would make sense
to someone looking from afar,
standing on the firmest land,
assuming that a recollection,
most precise,
would be the same
as having the experience I've had.

Plot is overrated.
Plot is the suppressed fire
of Quetzalcoatl's
Dark Mirror.
(Suppressed rhythms
and music as well).

Music in text is
synchronous
with incandescent imagination.

A Perfect Day

Let me put it otherwise.
Pick a day.
Any day.
It's a beautiful day.
A perfect day.
You wish you could relive it.
What if you could?
It would be like having
a perfect recording device,
a video device,
able not only to store
every visual impulse caught between

> your eyelid
> and the centre of your eye
> but in the centre of your eye
> every moment

every timbre of every sound
every beat pounding your chest
so you scream aloud
every whiff of every smell and
every last vibration
of every last touch and sound.

Wouldn't you jump at the chance of reliving
every select moment of your life?

That's what the Inquisitor,
his witches and priests promised us.

Utopia.

An Euclidean one.

A perfect replay.
A forever replay.
A mirror-soul replay.

A mirror-soul was such a perfect device, an
AI device.

And yet, such a thing would ~~erase~~ its very sense
of being a replay in the first place.

Because it would erase the connection
between

the moments of time you lived   and the very act of
you remembering them.

No self, then.   And no other, then.

Because there would be no
now   and   then.

What about love, then?

We love because,
and only because,
we can lose what we love.

It hurts.
I should know.
After all,

I lost the one I loved.
I lost my mother & father.
I lost my friends
in the last bombardment.

But I rather live the next five centuries in pain
than never to have fallen in love,

                              in
                              the
                              first place.

At least
the Spirit of Place
is a more benign one
than the Spirit of Race.

This Wouldn't Be a Story

This wouldn't be a story
if it had
no now
and
no then.
No beginning and no end.
But let us not confuse that with reason and its unfolding.
Nor with matter,
otherwise inert,
and its formation after a fashion, an order, or an intention.
All
       I
            have
                 is
                       frag
                              ments.

Scattered p-i-e-c-e-s.
Sound samplings.
Beats,
bits of a broken mirror.

Memories,
moments,
and events.

Back then there was me.
I was her, my back against the wall,
pinned to the floor of a council state flat in ExLondon
by police
and an inquisition witch
for being a bitch

to my mother
and not following their manners and creeds.
For listening to abuela
her fanciful stories
and to Bowie.

For being visited by the ghost of my father,
and falling in love with a Muslim neighbour.

They disliked my listening to black music.
And, most of all, my reading books,
which were forbidden,
Replaced by downloads.

They pinned me down.
So, I lit a fire within me.
The suppressed fire
of a dark mirror
                    In sync
with rhythm & music,
                    In sync
with incandescent imagination.

I lit
a dark flame,
an all-consuming fire.
And then I ran,
I ran like hell.

Took a Muslim sister with me.
I loved her.

At the river port, we said our farewells.
"I'll find you, in whatever form, one day,"

she said.

But I lost her.
When I took to sea.
To see.
Foresee to really see.
What they don't want us to see.

Or was it the other way around,
to unsee?

In the end,
an end I couldn't foresee,
the witch came after me and her
and all our friends.

Unleashed a mighty beast, made of subtle vapour,
or air.

She worked for the Great Inquisitor,
that bitch,
in the Home Office.

They say
"tru$t u$"
But they wish
to break us
kill us
hate us.

To take from us the elements
of story
stored
in the cargo bay of our ship at sea,

which we were taking across the ocean sea
to the free people of the library at The Garden
for them to free themselves
To see and tell stories again.

Liberation.

That is the goal
Such is the aim,
still.

Tell? I cannot tell, for we have lost the elements of story.
They were taken by the witch.
Where?
I cannot see.
I've lost my sister, my love,
my friends,
my mirror & soul.

Perhaps also my imagination
and the will to live.

It all happened one night.
The night of the world.

They came.
Took us by surprise. Put us under siege,
fired their missiles,
at our homes,
our schools,
and our hospitals.

Said it was in self-defence.

And all the media said the same.

I lost my eyes & sense.

When I came to consciousness again,
I was stranded at sea,
alone,
unseen.

My friends, my name, my mirror and soul were
nowhere to be seen.

So, please.
Do not ask my name. For there's
no word for it.
Do not ask for my story.
It hasn't happened yet.
Do not ask what happened to me.
I can't tell you.
Not yet.
Ask, instead,
where do words,
and tricksters,
and djinns,
and girls
that can light fires like me,
where do they come from?

Where do I have to go
to find the elements from which stories are made?

To allow for the return
 of the sunlight
of the tales

of survivance
to the heart of the sun
for it to shine upon this world
and her moon
now in darkness and despair.

"Hope is a thing with feathers,"
my father used to say,
repeating the words of a forgotten poet.
But it is worse.
Hope is trapped in a jar,
in the dark.
So that's where I will start.
Where all stories start.

In the dark.

Things to be Found in the Dark

Isolation.
Loneliness.
Desolation.
Blood and the things of blood.
Animals acting like men.
Such as trickster Crow & Raven.
That boygirl makes the world.
Men acting like animals.
Such as Coyote, the Djinn,
or Compay Anansi,
the spider,
who can web stories & shape-shift,
and girls who light fires.

Memories not monuments.

These are the things to be found in the dark.

Story of Hu

I

Llegó aquí entonces la palabra.
Tepeu, the Crow,
and Gucumetz, a shape-shifting Coyote,
sometimes a Spider,
came together in the dark of night.
They spoke in pictures
for words had not been created yet.
Dwelling on the matter
they agreed to bring together
their thought
and the sounds
Of heart & breathing.

Thus, storytelling began.

The relation of relations
of how everything that was in suspension
never was
because nothing ever is in suspension
and never has been in such a state of negation
all still
all silent
all quiet
for there's no such thing as
empty extension and therefore
no caves & no holes on the surface of the earth
or at the bottom of the sea.
No animals over it
or beneath it.

No fish
no jaguars or tigers
no stones or trees.
No manifestation of the face of the earth.

Sólo el pájaro de fuego que vuela sobre el mar del ahora y el
después y lo observa.

Only the sea of Crow's thought and Coyote's sky sound.

Nothing was related to anything in itself
but to something else.
So, there's nothing in itself
standing still on its quiet own being.

The bird flies over the water
rolling backwards in parts and beats at times
jumping from parts to axion waves
that reverb saturate
the music scale
without repetition or delay
without anything moving in between
only cut-in and overlay.

It carries Tepeu and Gucumetz,
in the sense that movement
is not something that happens to gods,
humans,
or things,
but rather,
gods,
humans,
and all things,
down to their innermost parts or beats

are something derived
from our observations of movement.

It doesn't mean they do not exist.

In the water
rolling backwards in parts and beats,
at times surrounded by the dark,
Tepeu and Gucumetz observed a great commotion.
A trickster djinn
in battle with a girl
who had no name
being trapped in a jar.
A witch fleeing the scene
with the things that can only be found in the dark.
She opened a hole at the bottom of the sea
onto the other side,
the backroom side,
the not-yet side.

Tepeu and Gucumetz saw this
through the eyes of the bird of before times.
Which was the only thing that could be observed
and observe in the dark
because of its silver eyes
and the splendour of its green and blue plumage.

Quetzal.

II

Tepeu and Gucumetz are called mother and father.
They are rolled into one.

Their nature is that of thought and rhythm sound.

This is how the sky came to be.
But also, the heart of the sky.

They wondered:
How can this be?
How can we tell the others
what we have seen
if there are no words still
and the witch has hidden in a hole in the dark
all the things that can be found in the dark?

So, they decided to weave together
Crow's thought and Coyote's sound
and this is how the word came to be.

The living word.
The heart of the sky.

No manifestation or destiny.
But
worlding word
or figuration.

A memory
coming from the same subtle matter
that girls who can light fires are made of.

Una mujer de maíz.

She will face the dark
and the heart of the dark
and in the dark of night

she will fight death itself
to return the elements of story
for the coming of another_kind.

This is no manifestation,
but the worlding & figuration
of Tepeu and Gucumetz,
which is always incomplete
and must be reanimated
time and time again
which must be rendered into music & song
for it to be sung
so that time can continue to exist
and for worlds to exist

In time.
Of time.
Against the times.

And for all to know
that her name is incomplete,
but not lost.

And she's now called Huracán.

El país de la penumbra

This is the journey of Hu girl to the land of the dead.

A memory of how she brought back

                          the gift of the storier.

For stories themselves come from darkness.
They are gifts from the dead.

She was born
you might recall
with the gift of fire
at a time when light
had been robbed

                    from the world

and the first men drowned.

The skies were cold
The sun hid underground
obscured by gas clouds
the cities doomed and domed
covered the faces of the moon and the sun
drowned the men of clay and wood.

In this world,
Vucub Caquix ruled
over the few places
spared by the great heat and deluge.

Of silver were his eyes
shining dark like obsidian mirrors

>without light
capturing the souls
of the drowned
to adorn his teeth.

He would send an inquisitor witch
to rob Hodoo Girl of her name,
the land of ancestors,
her mirror and soul,
for his ambition was to swallow all others

>in his being.

Then came the word,
a figuration and worlding of Coyote and Crow,
in the drowned world,
and with it the girl.

The girl that lit a fire.

Having survived
having lost her mirror and soul
she renamed herself
Hu/Huracán/Hunah pú.

She was the first.

The second,
made of the same subtle matter
words
and firegirls
are made of,
we shall call Ix or /x/

Ixbalanqué.

As in Latinx
Or Malcolm X.

Trapped inside a jar,
Ix was washed up
on a beach
in an unknown coast
on the other side of the sea.
Found a fire kin,
Coyote
who shape-shifting into a feathered serpent
took the jar
(from the white witch)
down into a cave
at the entrance of hell
into the place they call The Backroom
so that it could be found by Hu girl.

Hoodoo Girl
Hu
now
Huracán,
fallen feather of a firebird,
drifted at sea.
She was washed up
on a beach
in an unknown coast
on the other side of the sea.
Found a fire kin,
Crow,
who once flew
with the chariot of the sun,

he's the harbinger of healing
heatwaves
and axion waves

The lowest rhythmic interval
becoming music or wave.
An axion mass scale wave.
It acts
sometimes
as if made of billiard-ball parts
and other times
sloshing like watery waves.
Waves coming together in rhythmic overlay
to create a super wave
that no archive can place
in a final resting place.

Crow spoke to Hu
the only way he can.
He
spoke in pictures,
of the healing that could only be found by a girl
down underground
and of the things that only in the underworld
can be found.

Here. Now. I am here.
Hu said,
as she moved backwards
into the cave
downwards
into the land they call Xibalbá.
The Land of the Dead.
El País de las Masacres.
El País de la Penumbra.

Story of All Stories

Everyone knows that
djinn,
tricksters,
and girls
are made of **sub**tle fire.

A **sub**terranean incandescence,
simultaneous
with image

                                                   &

                                        the rhythm of a beat.

                                        No longer a **sub**stitute metaphor
                                        But the bract which **sub**tends
                                        And enfolds all literature.

No one knows where such matter came from.

How it came to be

                                        superpositioned

                                                        and
                                intertwined

in the atom heart
of djinn and girls with exploding hearts.

Suppose it's subterranean.

I mean,
how they made a secret pact

to go down underground
moving sdrawkcab and
d
 o
  w
   n
    w
     a
      r
       d
        s
to defeat the lord of death
hidden in the dark
and bring back light,
a **trans**itive medium,
between heaven and sky.

Music/makers whistling
through a window,
located in a corridor,
in Lord Death's palace,
in ancient El Dorado,
subbed darkness for
the wind sound of a whistle
or the skin sound of the pound drum
that in such an instant becomes,
a secret medium of **trans**itive density.

I emphasise **trans**, **sub**tleness, and **density.**
As though a beat or a chord
exists within that window,
the window that goes down & out
-within the density of the window (let us say)

and the skin of a drum.
So, the window,
located in a corridor,
in Lord Death's palace,
in ancient Xibalbá or El Dorado,
becomes a medium of transitive density
as the chord & the beat fire,
(so)
to speak,
and their whistle is transformed
as it passes through the window
into an eruption of
Fantastic
Critique & disruption
light & music
that lives
within the heart of subtle things.
Such as word,
wind,
whistle,
downward bound
through a cave or a window
and into the text of reality.

It fires,
the word fires,
in sync with the music & the beat.

And thus appears,
in sync with the beat & the music,
the lightning bract
That subtends the flower and bark of a tree.

It is the flower, the tree, and the trunk

of Continental Liberty.
The long continental
literary tradition
of literature in the Americas.

Such tribal literatures are the tree,
the oldest literatures.
They *are* the canon.
But we don't see the tree,
because the things of **subt**le density
at its root
remain obscured
by an idea of
Order
&
Exhibition
&
Publication,
the logic of the museum & the archive,
in which everything would have
its final resting place
or no place at all.

Such was/is
the utopia
of the Big Inquisitor
and his witch in the Home Office.

But in the atom heart
of djinn and girls with exploding hearts
there is an alliance.

An old alliance
between music & text.

As old as the tradition of
Continental Liberty.

Which is simultaneous
with the incandescent imagination
With which all the stories are made.

This is their story.
The story of that alliance.
The alliance between a djinn and a girl.
Hu & Ix.
And of how
they went underground,
to bring back the exploding sun of stories.

If so,
it is also
the story
of all the stories that have ever been made.

A feather
from the bird of before times
&
from the bird of after times
falling from the straight line.

A declining clinamen.

A bass beat at the top of the song.

Beat. Beat. Beat.

T...
          ...th

...the

There was, back
                    then
no light over the face of the earth.

There was no sun.
Only the night of the world.

And no word
only the thought of Crow
and the shape-shifting music sound of Coyote beat
which
he cuts-in and overlays
at random
in his midi mixing machine
to make mighty mountains
of
magma
        move

                    sideways,
backwards

and
↓
  downwards

where worlds wane and wither,
worlds woven,
winds wandering wildly
until the girl who fell from the straight line,
in declining clinamen,
like the bass beat at the top of a song,

comes to let understanding stop
at what cannot be understood.

An incandescent sky,
in sync with the imagination,
wound and unwound,
would then
shine again.

But there was also a being,
a vain,

       and **vain**glorious
being
named Vucub Caquix

                  el pájaro de fuego
                  a firebird

hovering high over the heavens
       high over the holes

                  that molten magma
                  coming from the feathers
                  of the firebird

had left

                  while it crossed between
                  now and then.

It all happened after the first men drowned.
When the face of the world was covered,
and the face of the sun was covered,
and the face of the moon was covered.

And darkness reigned all around.

Vucub Caquix said:

"Truly, there were only the men who drowned.
Now I will be great and grand and master
over/all that is left.
To me they will be bound.
Those ascending the stare
between my eyelid and the centre of my eye,
and those gone underground.
Those who already are,
and those who are but not yet.
For I will replace the shine of the Sun and the Moon
with the green and blue splendour of my plumage
quetzal.

Of slithering silver are my eyes
shining and shivering in the dark,
like emeralds.
They can see from Yucatán to Transvaal,
like the mirrors without light that captured the souls of the
drowned.
My teeth encased in gold and diamonds.
My wings and body bright from afar,
like the Sun
and the Moon
made of fire,
they can turn all into ash.
Great is the extension of my sight,
and greater still is the illuminating distance of the light
coming into my silvery eyes."

So said the bird of fire,
even though his sight could only extend to the horizon line,
projected onto the imaginary divide between heaven and the
earth.
The earth

that looks flat from where the bird was.

The firebird was ambitious.
He believed his sight could extend over the night of the world.
He believed he could swell the world,
with his own being.

That is why
he is to be killed
by the twins
Hu & Ix
whose very essence emerged
out of the subtle matter
that the universe
and the feathers of the bird
are made of
light & sound
waves and particles
not words
but pebbles of w-o-r-d-s

                        and

                                syl-la-bles

not letters but fragments of
l
e
t
t
e
r
s
falling like feathers
in declining clinamen
or the subtle matter beyond atoms
and in the spaces between them.

as in JNN
نَجّ or نَجّ
which means to hide,
to be made invisible,
beyond the vanished point of perspective and sight.

Banished to the dark.

It means to change or adapt.
And refers also to what has been hidden down underground
or at the bottom of a jar.
So, to reveal it,
bring it to the light,
the participant observer must invent
A different way of seeing.

A different figuration
a worlding
an image-system
capable of

    sensing
    and making sense
        otherwise.

Not a method or its reason
but a utopia that doesn't look like one.

The trick is
to think what you sense
   &
to sense what you think.

Such is the way.
There's no magic in it

but simple decency
inherited by those who descent from frag
ments
of history,
not from judgmental
statements,
but rather,
from
stammerings,
stone stamens of ruined monuments,
staggermoments
of subtle matter
before words or solemn speeches   before heroic tales or novels
could be said or performed   could be put on a page
       and in the space between them
       where can be found the signs of the possessed
بوتچه   majnún
on the other side of
janna   ةّنج،
which is The Garden
   and
چذسذ   janín
which is the unborn,
      unhatched,
unfinished and incomplete becoming.

Life in its early stages,
the life of the word
before words or solemn speeches could be said
or performed.
Before heroic tales or novels could be put on a page,
performed no longer on a stage
but in the stage of the readers' mind
      and in the space between words

                              which is the night of the world
out of which the life-giving,
wind-rising,
storm-riding,
fire-starting
girl named Hurricane
emerged into this world,
together with the jinn,
and made a pact
to help women and men be reborn from maize
Together with their animals,
with birds and jaguars,
who carry in their backs the sun of the night,
composed of a sheath and a long distal blade
joined together by an auricle
so that the blade can bend away

                              from the stem,
                              change or adapt
                              to a hurricane
                              or a mighty rain.

Such was the secret pact
made
between the jinn and the girl.
Ginnaya and Jaini.
Who will become lovers, sisters, or twins,
Hu and Ix,
Hurricane and Sex.

Memory & Sex

This is the story of their pact.
A lovers' pact.

This is the story of the ruin
of the Lords of Xibalbá
in
the dark place.
And of the fall of Vucub Caquix
at the hands of two sisters,
twins,
or lovers.

Hu   the girl
                    and
Ix   the jinn

                        Hurricane   and   Sex

Who were truly godly,
for they were subtle matter.
The pebbles of words
with which to sense and make sense
in a way that no clever device
made by men can
not yet
because to sense and make sense
is to differentiate
between the rules applied to a case
and that which is the case,
the experience of coming to be,
of the world,

and of the life of the word
outside those rules.

Before words and solemn speeches could be
performed
alone and isolated
to persuade foot soldiers to carry out
the Inquisitor's command of
blood and the things of blood
and bring displacement and desolation
during the apotheosis of war.

Before heroic stories and novels could be put on a page

                                                 sold

and performed in the mind of a reader
isolated
alone
in a desolate place
trying to escape blood and the things of blood
(el país de las masacres, este país)
where animals act as men
men act like animals
and the things that can be found in the dark
are no longer

                                    told

but drenched in blood
to sustain the reign of terror
and maintain the sovereignty
of wealth & riches.

This is the story of our ruin and fall.

And of a pact
made many moons ago

how many
no one knows
between a girl and a jinn
to snatch those things
from the Dark Lords.

This is also a memory,
and like all memories
you wish you could relive it
exactly as it was
only you can't
because reliving that memory
exactly as it was
would mean ~~erasing~~
the difference that permits it
to be a memory
of what it was.

So, this is the story
and the memory
of the subtle matter
that permits
the existence of memory and story.

Trans

I

A subtle matter
A difference only.

A small difference
between the memory of a day
any day
a perfect day
the one you wish you could relive it
and the lived experience
to contrast it.

A small difference.
But one that makes
all the difference

between us and the clever machines we make
between the pedantic precision of rules
their application
by those who claim praetorian,
inquisitorial status
those who wish to swell the world
with their own being
to the point of proclaiming
the repetition of a scene of the past
exhaustive of any novelty to come.
To the point of proclaiming
the security of the burrow
and its stillness paramount.

Let's call that precision forensic, on the one hand.

On the other hand,
the suspension of that forensic proclamation.
And of the inquisitor's judgment.
At the abarian point between field forces,
which appears
in the space created
by breaking apart
the precedents and orders
given by those who burn crosses,
in the name of securing the mole's burrow.
Fantastic precision,
We call it.

Fantastic precision
of the suspension (of judgment)
of hesitation (when the order to kill is given).
To stop the chain of their commands.
To push back against their inertia.

And save lives in the process.

Those who burn crosses
practise a magic
that isn't memorial,
neither music nor the shaman's performance art.
But a monument,
pacifying in its stillness.
Ineffectual
re
presentation
of the sacrifice
of an animal acting as man

a goat
or a lamb
a burrow perhaps.

Those who burn crosses
declare that instant a hinging moment,
the key moment,
the instant in which fate,
dead set in the past,
becomes manifest,
and bears being repeated,
again and again,
for all time.

Again, for all time,
is the same as
the stillness of the burrow.
The joy of the burrow.
The pleasure of the burrow.
The happiness of the burrow which
is the same as
the joy procured by burrowing.
The pure joy afforded by moments of
pure silence and stillness.
Death.
The sheer pleasure of watching
still images projected in the mind,
without music or dance,
and the infinite pleasure
of keeping watch over the burrow's entrance.
So, no foreign stranger can come here.
Contain them
Keep them at bay
Exterminate all the brutes!

Such is the command
of those
that work forces
The same ones who burn crosses
The same who find infinite pleasure
Keeping watch over the burrow's entrance.

They say:

freude
glück
genießen
arbeit macht frei

II

We refuse to.
We revolt against their command.
Their imitation of motion.

If that imitation of motion
exhausts novelty,
the alternate voice & sound   (Coyote)
of an alternative thought   (Crow)
becoming beat & voice
          rhythm & song
          music & dance,
then its message is
one of death:
don't move
don't take apart
don't doubt or criticise
don't refuse
don't dare to hesitate, change, or revolt.

And its happiness
the stillness of
what just is.
The belief that work
shall set you free.

We are led astray here.
To confuse what just is with justice.
That confusion paves the way to the camps
and the killing fields
of the apotheosis of war in the lands of our childhood.

No motion,
no sub,
no beat,
no trans.

Such dark magical worldview
is the point of spectacle.
And of the world,
the night of the world,
in which we live now.

A world
inherited from the Fourth Lateran Council,
and the feast day of the Eucharist.
Imprinted upon us
every Sunday of childhood.
When we were told
that the communion wafer, when blessed,
comes back as the body
of an animal acting as man
a goat
or a lamb

perhaps a burrow.

It matters not whether you believe or not
(that)
such a thing is possible.
The point is not
faith or belief.

But the fact that we are called upon
to act
as if we still believed.

For no one believes today
in the same way
the crowds of Liège rushed to witness the elevation
of the Host
by Urban IV in 1264.
For them it was not a matter
of letting yourself go,
or taking a leap of faith,
as they say today.
For them it was a matter of reality.

It is different for us.

If for us
reality has become spectacle.
If in the dark
shadows have come alive.
It is because
the thing called Evil
has come back as a new problem.
We no longer believe in it,
but we feel anxious to let go of our crouches,

grow up,
stare into the abyss,
enter the burrow,
and dare to
go down underground.

So, we prefer to act as if we still believed
in such things as Good or Evil,
and the flames of Hell,
so far as we do not have to enter or experience it.

We prefer to act as if we still believed
in the apotheosis of the Host
so far as we do not have to experience
the apotheosis of war in the lands of their childhood,
so far as we do not have to entertain the memory
or what it was like to be a child,
a boy or a girl,
back then,
when the paras came,
and the basketball field
became hell.
The site of a massacre.

So far as blood and the things of blood
remain in the dark,
buried underground,
under a pyramid of corpses,
in the mass graves of my childhood.

I would have to transform, then.
First into a donkey or a camel.
Then into a lion.
Finally, into a child.

To dream up new domains
and other beginnings.

To fight those who adjudge history in the as if way.
The monumental historians,
who still write as if all the Evil in the world
was the result of a few Evil Men,
and the result of the indifference
of the fewer Good Ones.
Who failed to act in the critical instant.
Who failed to measure in that instant
and to understand
what cannot be measured or understood.
Motion or change in an event,
or a thing as it is in itself.

The monumental historians
who still write as if
we could sense and make sense
or control
the forces at play
in an instant of change
pass judgment
on that September day
when bombs started to rain
fire over the presidential palace
and President Allende thought
of leaving his body behind
instead of waiting for certain death.

For them
Allende's
suicide is a failure to act.
They may even associate it to destiny and context,

read it as a symbol,
or a mark
of destiny becoming manifest
present in the body of
a man acting as an animal.
As if President Allende in his burning palace
were
a sacrificial lamb.
The proverbial scapegoat.
Even a burrow.
Or the price others have to pay
for Vucub Caquix to keep his burrow safe.

Monumental historians
are really theologians.
And bad ones at that.
For they proclaim the eternal duration of an instant.
They explain events
in terms of the purpose they serve.
And confuse context
with a question of laws of progress
or forces of design,
even though they themselves
no longer believe in such things,
because we no longer can.

Not in the same way as the people of Liège.

III

Those who view reality the as if way,
the monumental way,
declare:
If only we could call out

the evil women and men
who dream of rupture and revolution,
bring them to the dock
of history as tribunal,
kill them before they act,
or measure & calculate,
with the help of clever machines,
the moment of their act,
pre-empt their position,
ponder with forensic precision,
the relative force of the antagonism
engendered by attempts
to bring about historical novelty.

As if
this mediation was the only true representation
As if
negotiation did not require taking
the position
of the other,
to see oneself
through the enemy's eyes,
no
Here, I am here.

Then, at last, they say,
the inquisitor theologians,
the judges of history,
the builders of monuments
& monumental(l) utopias,
then all will be well.
The world or the republic will be pacified,
and utopia will be upheld
at last.

The utopia of order, that is.

One without memorials, only monuments.

Such is the utopia of the Grand Inquisitor,
Vucub Caquix.

IV

Hence, the pact made
between the girl and the jinn.

Hu said to the wind
hopeful that an echo of her words would reach the jinn
We fail to see
really see
the ineradicable nature of that constant,
the erosion of the present that no one can resist,
but which endows life
and the attachment you and I make in it
here and now
with all of their value.
Better to leave,
than seating still
and wait for death.
That is freedom.
And love.
We move, we struggle to be free, we love
because, and only because,
we can lose.

Dream

I

She moved.
Hu moved,
backwards and downwards,
quickly passing a steep
                    stair
rivers and barrancas
sailing across
ascending the
                    stare
between the eyelid
and the centre of the eye
of Firebird,
passing those they call mojay.

Beyond,
a river of blood
a river of fire.

Hu
got out
and down.

She came upon a crossroads.

The Black One.
The Red One.
The Green One.
The White One.

Crow
went down each road.

In the first he found nothing
In the second he found nothing
In the third he found nothing
In the fourth he found a dream.

A dream of whirlwind,
two lovers,
and the underworld

In the dream
the heavens roared,
the earth shook,
the mouth of hell opened.
There stood a man-bird,
leading the way
to the house from which
none who enters returns.

There's a place there, he said,
where people seat in the dark
eating dust and ash.

There's a place there, he said,
for the great kings of the earth.
Their crowns put away,
they are now slaves
in the house of dust.

There's a place there,
and he pointed to it with his finger bone.
There,

seated on a throne
was the Khan of the Dead
and squatting beneath her feet
the recorder of deeds
keeper of the Book of the Dead.

"Who has brought this one here?"
The Khan said
looking down at Hu
from her throne
in the bowels of the earth.

II

A youngling, a jinn
made of matter so subtle
subtler still than the wind
wakes up in the bottom of a jar.

His heart pounding.
He was she.
Now was he.
Boygirl thought of the one who had cut the chains,
thereby releasing him
from servitude to the witch,
as his lover and sister.
He thought of Hu.
He thought of the moment when the inquisitors captured
in the river of time
a mirror-soul in transit.
He thought of their encounter at sea,
and of the pact they made to struggle so they could be free.

Rather than being sent back to the burrow

they would leave,
leave their body,
imagine a different one,
instead of waiting for death.

Back then
He was she.
Now was he.

Back then,
it had taken ten agonising days for her to die
trapped inside a jar.
Inconsolable,
for she had promised
to meet her sister again
somewhere in Spain.

She wept,
and as she passed away
she left her body behind
to become a boy
and send word to Hu girl
to come rescue him.

III

Crow came back with a dream,
and a message within the dream:

Your sister
no longer her
calls for you
to join him
in the land of the dead.

Here

Who brought this one here?
asked the Khan at the gates of Hell looking down on me.
I decided to leave my body instead of waiting for death, I said.
The Khan took pity on me, came down and began to show
me everything that men have experienced. Sorrow and wealth.
Happiness and greed. Fortune and misfortune. What would
you take? I'll take stories with me. On one condition, said
the Khan at the gates of the Land of the Dead. That you give
Crow your eyes so you may listen, get others to listen and as
they listen dance to the beat, the bass, the night, for poetry is
music not light. Here. You shall be the first storyteller.

Episode 2. Down In a Hole

Blindness

In all the stories
characters of great wisdom
are often blind.

Or the storytellers themselves
are blind.

It is said that Tarvaa,
the first storyteller,
was blind.

It is said Homer was blind.

It is said that nearing the end of his life,
the Great Homer of the Caribbean
lost his mind,
it went dark,
and in darkness he read the stories of an unknown writer.
Listening to them for the first time
he danced to their music for the first time.

What is the meaning of blindness?
What does it tell us?

Some say it tells us
that stories are a way of seeing,
seeing without eyes.

Others say it tells us
that stories are not about seeing,
that poetry is not made of light,

but music.
A bass-soaked relay
that comes
sometimes in parts,
sometimes in waves
to those who can no longer see or wait.
For stories themselves
come from the darkness.
They're gifts from the dead.

Anti-epic of Gilgamesh

I

Here. I am here.
In the remotest mansions
to find and awaken my brother sister,
duende,
grope after it
in blindness,
wrestle with it
in darkness,
draw near it,
climb together
to places where mountains fuse together into a yearning
of sound
superior to their visible manifestation.

Here I hear the earth shaking.
Trembling as two peaks stretch all the way to heaven
and their bases fall far below the surface.
Here seats Utnapishtim,
the raw poet,
listening with careful attention
to a runaway resonance dilation
that extends from the great flood of old
to the quantum suspension
in the garden of the sun.
Where he was given the gift of life
everlasting,
but only
for as long

as he kept listening.

Here I asked Utnapishtim:
what does he listen to?

Perhaps it's the music of Coyote,
shape-shifting
into a spider,
into
Archie Shepp
doing a saxophone solo
featuring
Raw Poetic &
Damu the Fudgemonk.

The composition slides away from the proposed,
a declining clinamen.
It comes back
a shocking wave
to cultivate another voice
a voice that is alter

        other

than that proposed by one's intention,
angular,
oblique,
the obliquity of unbound reference.[3]

And therefore free.

---

[3] Nathaniel Mackey, *Paracritical Hinge* (Iowa City: Iowa University Press, 2018) 187.

Sound of the outside,
that everlasting outside
in which poets, storytellers, and musicians
enter into a concert
with the outside players
to learn the secret
of how to transition
between genres,
how
to become particle or wave
that reverb saturate
the horizon line of infinite space
and cause a delay
for those who can no longer wait.

In it
the sons and daughters of
all experience
all suffering
all pause
all death
can re
evaluate
and represent
all mysteries...

as they transit from
camel or donkey
to lion
back to child,
and in childhood,
imagine or hear
all mysteries as sound
migrating into the profane

without reservation or nostalgia
all the things that in the dark can be found
as I found them.
As sounds.
For a poem isn't light
but sound
sliding away from the proposed bounds.

If you and I listen to those sounds
and let understanding stop
at what cannot be understood
where the dark folds
into the next second
and the next one
that's where the things of the dark can be found:
the sound of the spirit
its velocity
not the speed of sound
but its interval.

Therein lies
the hesitant possibility of a future,
history as pause.
It slides away from the proposed
it gets into
it comes back
a shocking wave
shape shifting
into the cultivation of another voice
speaking more than one knew what.

This wooing of another voice
entering language and time
in such a way

that I
trans
move
a particle or wave
that reverb saturate
the horizon line of space
and causes a delay

The same darkness delay
that Gilgamesh
entered into
after crossing the gates of hell.

It became thick around him,
thicker still
for there was no light
nothing ahead of him
nothing behind him
but a beat
and at the end of it
another beat
silence interrupted
by the beat of steps
and steps of beat
climin up the mountain,
chillun,
didn't come here to stay
if I'm ever gonna see you again
[Brother Sister]
It'll be on judgment day.[4]

[4]Le Roi Jones, "Lines to García Lorca," *New Negro Poets: USA*, ed. by Langston Hughes (Bloomington, Indiana: Indiana University Press, 1964) 55.

II

Like Gilgamesh
I didn't come here to stay.
Like him
I came here to listen,
learn to listen
to the man who did not drown.

Learning to breathe.

Only he's now Archie Shepp
finishing his sax solo in
Learning to Breathe

He reaches for another breath
of air.
And the next one.
Raw Poetic picks up the mic

in the air

there is total silence,
until a tiny man,
one of those dancing manikins,
sarcastically murmurs into his ears
for him to repeat:

Beware the illusion of the timeless,
Fill your belly with good things…
dance and be merry,
feast and rejoice,
let your clothes be fresh,

bathe yourself in the music,
cherish the girl
that holds your hand,
and make her happy in your embrace
for this too is the lot of man.[5]

dance
dance again
take one step
and the next one

Here we care nothing about
        ability,
        technique, or
        skill.
Here we are after something else.[6]

Duende.

All that has dark sounds,
has duende.

III

Everything ends.
Palaces to do not stand forever.
Monuments crumble

---

[5] For the sources of these verses see 'The Dispute Between a Man and his Ba' and 'Three Harper's Songs [The Song from the Tomb of King Intef', both in *Ancient Egyptian Literature*, ed. M. Lichteim (Oakland: University of California Press, 2019) 207-14 and 244.

[6] Federico García Lorca, *Deep Song and Other Prose* (New York: New Directions, 1980) 45.

to dust,
the voices of kings and heroes stammer
and the long slender stamen
breaks.
All this is testament
to the passage of time.
Everything ends.

Upon hearing such dark sounds
coming from the mouth
of raw poet
Utnapishtim,
Gilgamesh recoiled.

Like me,
he too had travelled far for a secret.
Instead,
unlike me,
he heard truth
and summoned the courage to live it.

There's a thorny plant,
that flowers underwater.
The stamen of which
is said to heal
cure
restore youth.

Said to Gilgamesh the raw poet Utnapishtim.

Gilgamesh went down.
Deep
Deep
Down

Into the pit.
There he found it.
In the beat.
Such things as one can only find in the deep and dark.
Made his way back to the village of his childhood,
dreaming of eternal youth
happiness and joy.
The happiness of stillness.
He stopped by a cool water well,
but deep in the well,
 unseen by Gilgamesh,
there was a serpent.
Of scales so strong
they seem made of stones,
stamens as old
as a testament.
It smelled the sweetness of the flower,
grabbed it from the hands of Gilgamesh
and shed its skin to avoid been caught
at once returning to the deep.

Gilgamesh stammered.
No
No!
The flower was lost forever,
and as it happens to all who live,
he too
            will die
                    one day.

stones
stamens
testaments
and stammers

the voices of heroes and kings
their palaces
they too
      will pass
            one day.

Allow me,
architecture,
to go down this path
made of
sand
timber
ore
neon light
electricity all round
to fret
the store monuments of Man
with a stick.

Stammament

Allow me,
architecture,
to fret stammens with a little stick,[7]

Hu said.

Did you lift
stone above stone
over him?

Did you light
fire upon fire
upon him,
drowned him
and the world,
under an ocean of tears?

What kind of G-d would do such a thing?

To you
men have build
Stone above stone
Fire upon fire
Cathedrals of fire-crested gold
And in that gold
is
my brother's blood.

Let me have him.

---

[7] Pablo Neruda, *Heights of Macchu Picchu*, 57.

Let me have the brother
you buried here!

Ix Reborn

I cannot know
whether I live
or not
trapped as I am
in the bottom of a jar

set me free
leave my previous body behind
rather than wait for death
for
I can hear
punctuated sounds
of speech
the voice of my lost sister
/lover
/brother
a memory
reclaiming time as being
not of monument
or visuality
reclaiming life in words
to replace the image of progress along a straight line
imagined by those who work forces
against clinamen
against my sliding away from the proposed line

their burning of crosses
staggers
my motion and transition
from camel to lion to child
to time,

a new beginning
after staring into the dark

ascending that stare

retell my tale even if when I sing
my voice
stammers
involuntarily pauses as broken
voices
stamens
of time
or memory flowering into
testament
and testimony
to the dead
during the apotheosis of war
in the land of my childhood.

One pauses
flowers and stammers.
The other is unbreakable and made of marble.

Such is the difference
between memorial and monument,
between song or poetry and the hero's novel.

The latter has come to stand for an occlusion of novelty.

The former paves the way to a new beginning.

A telling needing to be continually retold,
it stammers
involuntarily pauses

retold and reheard like myrtle
stamens
of time flowering
in memory
of our resistant dead

Allow me,
architecture
to fret stone stamens
stammaments
monomonuments
staggermoments
marblestonetestaments
and break free,

reborn.

Memory (2)

Memory (is)
one (brief)
play (or)
experience (of)
temporality (that)
slowing (down)
lost (fiery)
spectres (of)
lost lives (can)
salvage (them)

Lost Lives

Here's to
the lost
the withdrawn
the exiled
the not yet known
and the not yet spoken

Here's to
slowing the time
of what has been said already
slowing it with a greater sense
of care
for the missing
to speed up the spirit
into travelling other dimensions
hidden from view
assist in the creation of a
holding environment
for self-transformation
building bridges
between the said and the unsaid

This entails a relation to
memory.
Within the holding environment,
or imaginary domain,
one
also draws into
play
a sense for past
experience...

which may figure a
temporality
of anti-violence, a
slowing
down... by repair... to keep in mind
lost
traces of that which is missing:
spectres of lost lives.[8]

To salvage them.

[8]Brandon La Belle, *Acoustic Justice* (New York & London, Bloomsbury) 17.

Ocean of Sound

"Once is maybe enough"
David Toop.

For you I have crossed
An ocean of sound

pushed it in our mouths pushed it
deep inside
all wrapped in ribbons[9]

of robbed dark memories
dubbed in ambient music.

I was inspired
by your breaking
previously tight divisions which seemed
unbreakable
between genres breaking down
which delivered
earthquakes
to my doorstep but then short changed
by my failure to foresee your dead
heart

---

[9] Pictures of You – The Cure.

now crossing mine in dreaded
despair or unlove not listened
to
even though I kept shouting fully formed
inbroken sentences unpacked
in tears making an ocean of sound.

Other Things to Be Found Underground

Darkness
Isolation
Desolation,

a place

Void of life

like a desert or an ocean
                        (of sound)

Loneliness

                        which can be found among a crowd
                        and does not require solitude
                        or aloneness

A hundred years of

                        men behaving like animals
                        animals behaving like men

Queequeg casting runes
Calchas envisioning a plague,
                        blind prophets

Captain Ahab nailing to the mast a Spanish piece of eight
King Agamemnon capturing the women of Apollo's temple,
                        blinded men

These are other things
to be found underground.
They make stories

Fly off the ground.

On the other side,
sister
brother,
lover,
The Garden.

Future Imperfect (Anti-Novel Manifesto)

I

Who are these foreigners coming to our country?
They bring their words and games
to play with our heads,
they show no shame
even though the pictures they bring with them
seem to us unrecognisable,
and cannot be read.

Don't they know
literature begins with letters,
and anything otherwise
is the ruin and relic
of a preliterary past?

Like the texts of sound and image
alive in sacred sites,
found throughout the native Americas.
Or the visual memory cues of pictographic inscription,
and the lights of Andean khipu,
that show Don Misael and his people ways of voyage
across the abyss of dereliction
left by the paramilitaries when they destroyed his lineage
and imposed the Grand Inquisitor's vision.

Didn't these immigrants see the news? Didn't they die in the
crossing?
Go tell them we, the lords of this land,
The Grand Inquisitor
of the Lords of Xibalbá,

call on them to perform
according to our conventions
And the word of our Lords
in the theatres of Laws.
Tell them
in seven days
we shall send our
Home Office team
to play against the foreign twins a game we call 'The Harrowing'.

It is a simple game,
a forensic game,
an interrogation game.
Its final aim:
acceptance of the outcome
as their fate, final place, and name.

II

Seven days later,
the twins
Hu and Ix
came before the officers
in the Home Office's dark house.

Here is your sentence, said the officers.
You can read it,
realise your lives are over,
your fate inevitable,
and succumb.

And when you leave this office,
you can thank your interrogator,
for branding in your skin

the wisdom of our commandments,
the convention of our creed and manners,
And His Word:

There were two in paradise,
And the choice was offered to them:
joy without freedom, or freedom without joy.
There's no other choice.

The rules of the game are quite simple,
said the officers to the twins Ix and Hu.
Do not speak in pictures,
we will only hear believable stories.
But we cannot believe you.
For we declare your nature Evil.
Sex and Hurricane.

III

Tell stories? Sardonically said a twin. I would if I could
but no longer can.
People no longer dare crossing the threshold
to the underworld,
where stories hail from.
We have lost the elements of poetry and music,
no longer know how to deal with mythic matter,
and only a handful of writerly poets,
in a handful of places,
can summon plebeian courage
to bring about new visions,
experimental objects of sound
or lightning essays.
This world has given up on the world of the Nohor,
damned dream-books and word-cinemas,

obscured their ongoing poetics
(despite their force continuing into this century)
and the life of the word.

Instead,
there are novels.
Perfectly crafted, perfectly marketed
best-selling novels.
Written with a mastery no one denies.
But can the euclidean vision of their linear narrative,
do justice
to our stopgap migrant condition?

Perhaps it can expose a secret or two
in the light of forensic judgment.
That there were two in paradise, and a choice was offered
to them:
Joy without Freedom or Freedom without Joy.
And that there's no other choice.

But such is the light of today's industries
of performance.
The churches of currency
which destroy the secret
in the moment of its revelation.
And if exposure destroys the secret,
as shaman Don Miguel says
from ancient Amerindian wisdom,
then how to bring about a revelation that does justice to it?

We say secret and we mean hidden truth,
and when you equate secret and truth like this
"it seems to me there's more than a hint

of mystery and fate working in cahoots."[10]

Consider theatre,
dialectics & dialogue,
first figured in the living language
of a poetry to be declared aloud,
the way one declares love,
dramatises an oath,
or declares it broken.
The way young Achilles swore to protect dark-eyed Chalcas,
bearer of doom prophecy.

Dialogue was relocated –
from theatre's stage
to the stage of the reader's mind.
Giving absolute reign to
the adult's imagination of
the child's imagination
which adjudged the latter
to be the fantasy
of children and innocent brutes
condemned to extermination,
thereby burying
the asymmetry of a different past.

We say:
let's bring *critique fantastique* back –
dream-books and word-cinemas,
the vision & world of the Nohor,

---

[10] Michael Taussig, 'The Adult's Imagination of the Child's Imagination' in *Aesthetic Subjects,* ed. by P. Matthews & D. McWhirter (Minneapolis: University of Minnesota Press, 2003) 449.

and the asymmetry of the past,
which moderns declared ruins and relics
forcibly displaced onto
a
homogeneous
empty space,
a museum exhibition,
archived in a final resting place,
supposedly to be protected from the perils of the present,
but in fact,
burned or banned when daring to imagine futures otherwise.

Imagined an instance of misrule and chaos
by the adult's imagination of the child's imagination,
inquisitors and officers
Forced us to abandon them.
They command
to
bow our heads
to the west where the sun sets
and accept as inevitable fate
that death triumphs
desire is betrayed
no joy without pain
and nothing can be reserved
For the coming days.

Lo, we unfold our darkness
and on this rock place,
this marble-like cold place,
Which is said to be our final resting place,
 a new pact we declare.
Laws of peace, of love, of cohabitation ... another way
For when the way is lost,

says the old Book of the Way,
there's alliance not allegiance.
When there's alliance, there's justice.
And with justice, the new rites and ceremonials.
Which are the end of loyalty and allegiance
to the single vision
of the Grand Inquisitor.

In the new pact, the poetries of
critique fantastique & masque
Would no longer be flattened into plot,
nor subjectivity be confused with
authenticity
or identity
or marble-like character.

We refuse to swear allegiance to the symmetry (of plot)
and to collapse all dimensions of literature
into those of
The homogeneity of the group,
inner space
& commerce.

IV

Tell stories? wondered the other twin. I would if I could.
but we K/c/ant.
People no longer dare crossing the threshold to the underworld,
where stories hail from.
We have lost the elements of poetry and music,
no longer know how to deal with mythic
matter,
and only a handful of writerly poets,
in a handful of places,

can summon plebeian courage to bring about new visions,
experimental objects of sound
or lightning essays.

We gave up on the inner life of the word,
gave up on the world of the Nohor,
relinquished our dream-books and word-cinemas.
Instead,
we have novels
perfectly crafted novels
written with a mastery no one denies. We have
televised news & melodramas.

But in these novels,
if a girl speaks to her dead sister
or a boy runs into the forest of ghosts
after the paramilitary set their house on fire,
if that boy or girl ran into
woods
or escaped by sea from dystopia
or fell through a hole underground leaving their body behind
to be preserved at the bottom of the sea
or in those
woods,
for tomorrow's sake,
rather than wait for death,
then they're adjudged
Backward
Or Brute,
And the decree is proclaimed:
Exterminate All the Brutes!

And if in that instant
their sister's lifeless body seeps up to them from beneath

and returns
to subtle matter
(how long is this instant?)
nuzzled in the crook of what once was their father's or
mother's arm
so that,
fist balled against
God
Earth
Sky High,
that boygirl weeps over bodies
in their House of Ice
his
her
mouth
agape behind a hurricane
unable to react
mute
not willing to compute
or relate the facts,
then that is judged not to be true
it isn't realism
couldn't count as hi-fidelity literature
nor be registered
as what may be considered believable.

Today's industry of performance
advises that the page or the camera be all-seeing.
The audience wants to see it all.
Not to struggle for liberation.
But only to matter.
All that matters, all that,
especially mattering.

All Lives Matter.

This is the panopticon of voyeurism.

To be realistic & believable,
today's industry of performance says:
set aside,
onto a backwards space & time,
the other things that might not pass the test of the forensic
eye
of the praetorian class
(a flick of the hand
a gesture of wonder or surprise
a fleeting glance at the lens,
and the take is rubbish).

V

The revolution will not be televised,
But our protest will be sampled.
A bass-soaked overlay
That reverb saturates
Black matter
Opening
To liberate
La frontera border en el fin.
A void vortex,
An open wound.
In the ironic gesture
Of native storier Charles Aubid
When he waived back his raised hand
To Judge Lord
Of the High Court
And refused allegiance

To those who had commanded to His People:
One King, One God, One Law.

VI

Consider Charles Aubid,
Native Storier
of the White Earth Reservation.

Many moons ago
no one knows how many
Charles Aubid,
wordsmith of the Chippewa nation,
declared by stories the preservation
Not the authenticity of his nation
but their survivance in native presence.

Before a Federal Court
in an autumn moon
more than
no one knows
how many
many moons ago,
Charles Aubid raised his hand.

He
listened to the Christian oath,
broken many times,
no one knows
how many,
many moons ago.
An oath
spoken
for the first time

in the language of the Anishinaabe
invented by Crow and Coyote in the time before time.

Charles Aubid waved back his raised hand
at US District Judge Miles Lord,
an ironic take on that oath,
and spoke of natural reason & continental freedom
figured more than
no one knows
how many
many moons ago
when Coyote and Crow
came together and for the first time
told stories
weaving together sound and thought.

Charles Aubid told stories
that afternoon
In the Court of Judge Lord.
From memory,
which he shared,
he said,
with all matter
shattered
by the manifest violence of the colonisers.
Hailing all that matters,
not just All Lives,
but Liberation & The Tree of Continental Freedom,
Charles Aubid opened for the judge his stories.

In his stories
a further person
figured from visual memory comes to presence.
Old John Squirrel,

a visual reminiscence
of when the elder spoke
of the right to wild rice harvest,
manoomin
they called it,
practised many moons ago
no one knows
how many
on the shores of Rice Lake in Minnesota.

As it was agreed with the officers of the US government
no one knows
how many
many moons ago
on the same shores.

Charles Aubid said he was there,
When Old John Squirrel
met with the Federal agents.
When Old John Squirrel
submitted to their harrowing
interrogations
When Old John Squirrel
responded from memory to their claims for evidence.
And he listened carefully
When Old John Squirrel
was told by the inquisition officers
that the White Earth Nation would always keep its rights
to harvest wild rice.

Charles Aubid told
All who listened
That afternoon
In the Court of Judge Lord

that the Anishinaabe always invoked their rights
by stories.

But they did not listen.

He told Judge Lord
that Old John Squirrel was there
in those stories
and by those same stories he was made present that day in
court.

But Judge Lord did not listen.
Not because he did not know.
But because he did not want to know.
Such is the Art of Mastery.

John Squirrel is dead,
Judge Lord said,
looking down on the Anishinaabe wordsmith Charles Aubid
from his judge's chair,
and you cannot say what a dead man said.

The Lord of the Court
Judge Miles Lord
could have heard
Aubid's testimony.
And listened
to that testimony,
in that testimony
the visual trace
and memory
of an agreement
spoken
many moons ago

no one knows
how many.

But what he heard that day in court was hearsay,
and therefore unbelievable,
Judge Lord said.

Instead of learning
and listening,
Instead of learning
to listen,
Judge Lord
sided with the Federal Attorney,
A Bureaucrat of the Burrow,
who had objected
that in accordance with the forensic precision
of inquisitorial procedure
only the law's provision
of equal (white) masks without presence
can be admitted
to be timeless
unchangeable
believable.

There's no room in the burrow for poetry or stories.

VII

The Harrowing Interrogators
The Burrowing Bureaucrats
Of the Burrow
the
Inquisition Officers
& Policeniaks

of the Home Office
The US Federal Agents
Judge Lord
The Lords of the Dark Place of Xibalbá
and the bird-demon named Vucub Caquix
are more than characters.

They embody The Architecture,
The Framework,
The Manners,
The Spectacle
& Creed
of a society.

They show to us what happens
when that society descends
into a cult of
Architecture,
Framework,
Manners,
Spectacle
& Creed

in which no room is left for poetic memory and stories.

If a novel cannot show us
that hidden reality
If it cannot show us an alternative reality
if it cannot make room for the rhythm of poetic memory
& the music of its landscape
if it sides instead with Judge Lord
& the Lords of the Dark Place
If it remains
deaf

To the stories of Charles Aubid
To the connection between the living and the resistant dead,
and builds
Instead
only monuments on the page,
all the worse for the novel
of this age.

No matter how loudly the novel declares itself
Realist.
No matter how hard it tries to address
the gaze of a disembodied audience,
self-referencing and distant,
each one of them holding
placards over their heads,
with their proper places,
property holdings
& CEO Heads.

If that novel
has nothing to say
about the continuance of the stories
Charles Aubid told the court
that afternoon,
no one knows how many
many moons ago.
If that novel
has nothing to say
about the appreciation of pre-existing wealth
Justified
As though it were an uninhabited continent
then
at the very least
the novel will have to be reinvented.

It would be best –
best for literature and for society if it stammers,
if the novel
fails
hesitates
giving us time,
time to think
time to time
The time
which is memory & life
which is what the life of the word is.
Living memory not silent monuments.

Stammers are resonances
allowing for time's transit
carrying the long past
on into a future otherwise
than it was.
Transforming that resonance
to make us pause and hesitate
its reverb moving in a wave
to make something happen in us
that can no longer wait.

Aesthetic ideas
they show us the way
principles or new beginnings
with the force to carry
The long past
on into and create
a future otherwise.

If they show the way to utopia,
it is not utopia as it is supposed to look like.

Certainly not the Grand Inquisitor's utopia.

If the word
[utopia]
is to be redeemed,
it will have to be
by someone that cannot be redeemed.

Someone like
Hu and Ix
who followed utopia into the abyss
[which yawns behind the Grand Inquisitor's vision
like the open jaws of the jaguar behind the King
in the painting by El Greco]
and clambered on
to the other side with their symbols and tricks.

The symbol which Trickster
embodies and keeps
within
is not a static one
not an unchanging one
not an authentic one.

There's no such thing,
only transformation
& motion.

If so,
let understanding stop at what cannot be understood.

That would be the highest achievement.

Wilson Harris

Consider Wilson Harris,
surveyor of the inner territory of Guiana
a prolific student
of the indigenous wordsmiths of the territory of Guiana
becoming the wordsmith of the territory of Guiana.

He declared by stories
the survivance & memory of such native presence
showed us
word-cinemas
and dream-spaces
drawn out from a dream-map
of uncanny spaces
in the interior of Guiana.

That is a high achievement,
figured in the eye of the Scarecrow,
appeared
or evoked,
in the head of Crow's relative,
                              Raven.

In The Tree of the Sun
he showed us London seen through other
                              eyescapes
he observed
that the equation of catastrophe with
        a specific hinging moment in time
is a convention
born
many moons ago

no one knows how many
though it can be seen already
in the tale of Oedipus
when the king strikes an old man in a dispute at a

c   r
        r   o
                    o   a
                            s   d
                        s

With that action
a prophecy is fulfilled.
The king has entered fate
            unchangeable fate
            inextricable fate
he's now subjected to fate's
praetorian precision
and timeless laws.

Such forensic precision
imagines symmetry
as a pact,
between Oedipus's act and the past,
its effects taking place in such a way
that place itself,
timespace,
is coerced.
It becomes consecutive and flat
and the king's motion in spacetime
a succession of points

rather than events –

final
fixed
fatal.

They can be forever divided
into ever smaller points
and yet there's no way
Oedipus will escape his past
just as there's no way
Achilles will catch up with the tortoise.

Bring your ingenuity toolbox,
measure that divide
calculate its extension
express it in numbers
zero or one.
Logically, as
this or that,
or as a Manichean divide,
them versus us;
measure it
or its performance,
mistake numerical succession
for a temporal pattern or destination
make it calculable
manageable
and ready to hand –
an uninhabited continent
out there for the taking
that someone will occupy.

Now flash forward a few centuries,

into our time of security and pre-emption,
obsessed with calculation
and with putting a prize
on the risk-variations of a flattened time.
Mistaking plot for reality,
teleology for history;
imagine that future
of even cleverer machines
and tighter prohibitions
liminal prohibitions
security repressions
over trans

...and there you have it,
that's the world Hoodoo Girl escaped from in Book 1

The adult's imagination
of the child's imagination.
A flattening of all dimensions
into those of the page
or the plane of representation
together with the Gothic ideal of presentation.

A flattening of all that goes into figuration

including
the flick of a hand   weaving
a gesture of surprise   wonder
a fleeting glance at the lens   worlding
which is what Coyote and Crow did
when they first put together thought and sound
brains
muscles
a hand (raised in ironic gesture at the lord of the ball court)

the expenditure of energy over time,
all that,
is flattened
to fit the dimensions
of page & commerce

just because, in theory,
you could go on cutting spacetime in half
and on and on
voyeuristically zooming in
forever and ever
on smaller and smaller
units of sliced time.

But when you try to frame reality
into the unchanging yardstick of judgment,
to grasp our everyday experience in spacetime,
to visualise those unchanging solids,
you will engender Euclidean utopias
that no one can touch
but can crush real lives.
In that way
we engender the very strangeness
that the blind Argentinian prophet noted,
time and again,
as he went down a basement in a flat
in Buenos Aires
a thousand years after the patron saint
of dialogue and dialectic.

The problem is
neither
dialogue nor dialectic
but the mistake

of trying to measure transformation and motion
in an object
or event
as it is in itself.

A mistake
which is common
to forensic novels
and monumental history
when turned into a convention
it is used as a yardstick
according to which
crisis or catastrophe
should be understood
as a hinging moment in time.

A moment
that can be grasped or precisely described.
Call it fate
or context,
that convention, that yardstick,
the symmetry of space and time,
leaves no space for asymmetry -
the past
the weird -
memory,
or the fantastic magic of a dispute at a crossroads.

And no room for stories or poetry.

That is the utopia of the Inquisitor,
Vucub Caquix
and the Lords of Xibalbá.

Episode 3. Standoff

The Trial

On our day in court
The Lords of Xibalbá
decided to subject us
to three further trials.

The House of Videodrome
The House of Knives
The House of Ice.

In them
many things could be found.

A desert
a vast ocean
the island of the Minoans with its labyrinth
                and the monster at its centre
Scorpion Men
A beast on the outside, a man underneath
or the very opposite
Jekyll and Hyde
roaming the streets of Edinburgh.

La isla de las muñecas en México
Dr. Moreau's island,
or the one in which Dr. Morel's machine
can capture a fugitive's soul
in a mirror soul
and project it
day after day
until it becomes reality
for the visitors of the island.

Hades,
Argentina under the military junta
or the neo-fascists who call themselves
libertarian.

The domed boroughs of ExLondon
after a century and a half
of neoliberal doom.

The land of the Khan
that Gilgamesh visited.

A vast digital ocean of sound
the bush of ghosts
the Pequod
La Jeté
the past present and future of Ebenezer Scrooge
the land of the Vikings
laid to waste in Ragnarok's wake.

The Morlocks' cave
the palace of Siddhartha
Dresden or Hiroshima
Bogotá ca. 1991
Xibalbá
País de la penumbra.

Videodrome (Found Poetry)

Forget Game of Thrones.
Time to kill off the elves and get weird,
I read on a post online.

Aren't we bored
to death
of the European mediaeval settings of
fantasy tv series
and videogames?

What about rpg games
set in a post-colonial world
where all surviving peoples
tremble and transform
into coyotes and crows
at the merest sight
of the tyranny that enslaved them?

No more Baldur's Gate 3.

Forget Game of Thrones.

Here's to Geralt de Rivia
drowning in his own shit

                              (acting)

Why not weirder places like
El país de la penumbra
or weirder characters like Huhnapú
                    (the character formerly known as Hoodoo Girl)
and Ixbalanqué

(transiting from sister to brother)
who become lovers
while venturing down in a hole
to find underground
the elements of story
and save the world from drowning?

Now, that would be something
Worth playing.

I'm sick 'n tired
of our tolerance for Eurovision-inspired
folklore,
and fucking Tolkien,
who,
while tattooed on my back
has entirely run out.

I get it.
We're beholden to this fucking
neon bitch
you-got-me-from-behind existing universe.

But let's be frank.
The world of Toril,
where the Forgotten Realms are located,
is one of the most boring places
of the entire D&D universe.

Especially when compared
to the wonderful dissonance & mess
of the planes of the void
between worlds
which make me wanna guess

if in the next Spelljammer campaigns
victory or success
could be measured less
by the number of magical beings
and spells,
and more,
by the quality of mindflayers,
bodyhorror,
and druids having sex
with clerics.

Who look like the Lords of Xibalbá
trying to destroy
me and my twin lover
sisterbrother.

And don't get me going
on the fucking multiverse.
It is a hypothetical collection
of potentially diverse
observable universes.
Did you not hear hypothetical?

As for comic books,
give me Batman's cave any day.

House of Knives
(Found Poetry)

I can't remember shit
past 10:30

What I don't know won't hurt me,
especially if I know how not to know it.

Give me a pack of 'rillos and a scratch-off lottery.
Here.
Life of the fucking party, eh?
Drunk as fuck.
You lose always, said the blind prophet.
There's always one of those in these stories.
Always one like this.
Yeah. That's it.
The chemistry of the chemistry means
I can't remember shit
past 10:30

I don't do that usually,
getting drunk as fuck,
I mean,
not
usually
deadely

But they're off cocaine 'n ketamine here
at the gates of Hell or the Glen in LA.

I rather smoke
a little weed and wait no more

for the fucking hero to appear.
I don't do that usually, deadly,
but in this place
they're off cocaine and ketamine
and I keep drowning in the asphalt
as I walk to the shop in The Glen in LA.
Or is it hell?

While I wait no more
for the hero to appear
I'll crack the goddamn door wide open
let the fire go
and mama is no longer.

Only an empty room
but I couldn't help crying
told my little sister you remind me of someone else,
y'know that,
and got on
escaped
got on with the tv show.
I ain't never had no little sisterbrother.
I still love him though.
Found him,
y'know?
We're on a quest to go back to the insanity.

House of Ice

In the House of Cold & Ice

(a wagon in the Train of Fire and Ice,
which Manu and his crew took from
Santa Marta and Bogotá)

my lover sisterbrother and I
faced ice

                for the first time

and a death squad

                for the second time

as we made our way
up north
having crossed the Rio Bravo

(read Stix)

from the south.

How's this, they aren't dead yet?
Asked the Lords of Xibalbá
To their border militias and home office bitches.

Then set the jaguars free,
to bring us to Ntu,
the point from which creation begins.

But before their predator's teeth
sliced us 'n diced us
we made them dance
'til we turned the house on fire.

This is now the house of blues 'n fire.

Here, first is the salad
then the meat
then the vegetables...
WAIT,
we said,
quoting Oliver Lake,
bring all our food at one time
and on the same plate,
bring
Dixieland
Be-bop
Soul
Rhythm 'n blues
Cool school
Swing & avant garde
Free jazz
Rock
Jazz rock
Drill and Grime

WHAT KIND OF MUSIC DO YOU PLAY?
they asked,
THE GOOD KIND,
we replied,
fooling once again
the Hound of the Underground
the migra and the repo men
with their jaguar teeth.
The bats,
and the vampire bat,
the one they call Camazotz,
which sucks the life out of all mankind

disguised as a Wall Street
suit 'n tie.

When they went to war
in the lands of our childhood
we got to hide ourselves
in the clubs underground.

In Barbarie &
The Backrooms.

To survive the apotheosis
of capital & war
in the lands of our childhood.

We were children back then,
spoke and did as children do,
hid ourselves
in our music & dance
to survive.

But now I'm all grown up,
so I showed my head
through the door
the day before
and the day after
we partied all night.

And it was cut at once
by the regime,
Camazotz,
the vampire bat,
disguised as ESMAD riot police
and the good people of Cali.

Are you awake? Is it morning yet?
You're all silent, Hu,
you don't hop,
slide or jump to their every command.
Which is all well and good,
but why did they call to the house
at this godforsaken hour
and not in normal office ones during the day, tell me that.
Listen to me love,
they'll ring back tomorrow
or the day after tomorrow
or the one after that,
and they'll say
we don't know what happened,
it was many moons ago how many no one knows.

Hu's body remains silent
as if standing before Ix
though his eyes have turned to the tv,
mute, couldn't answer.

I would have liked to say it's nine 'o clock,
it's ok,
but I couldn't 'cause I had lost my head.

We've been defeated and vanquished, Ix said.

He called all the animals,
all the performers
and all the dancers.

Aretha Franklin & Sun Ra
Coltrane & The Dixie Hummin Birds
Miles & Muddy Waters, same.

Depeche Mode
soda & the cure, same
… for there's no, i can't get no, no,
LABELS DIVIDE! SEPARATE
my head
but the sounds make it whole again,
not to separate the oral from the literary.
One music – diff feelings & experiences but same,
the total sound-mass sound-
hear (here) all the players as one.[11]

---

[11] Sources, cut-ins and samples from online music posts, liner notes and, principally, from Oliver Lake, "Separation", in *Ntu: Point From Which Creation Begins* (Arsita/freedom, 1976).

and all the birds sing bass

Guilléncollage

"

Quieren que estemos Muertos[12]
para adornar la casa del Gran Jefe
pero
los grandes MUERTOS... no mueren nunca.
No porque hayas caído
Tu LUZ será menos alta
Y no porque te QUEMEN
En calle y plaza, contra el PUÑAL, PECHO y coraza
hablar[emos] indiferentes
del SOL,
de la Lluvia,
o la tormenta
que nos desplaza.
Te entrego mi poema, algarabía
en lengua de piratas
donde todo el material habla
creaking the word algarabía
back to moorish Spain
with Federico García Lorca
noisy chatter between trabajar
duende
and Cuba
Federico,
Granada,
y Primavera.

Or improv jazz

---

[12] For the source of the verses sampled here, Nicolas Guillén, *Antología de la poesía cósmica de Nicolas Guillén* (Méjico: Frente de Afirmación Hispanista, 2001) 9, 22, 26, 33 and 49.

& hip hop
featuring Archie, Raw Poetic & Damu the Fudgemunk
creaking the improv into deep song
trip hop
carretón
of broken phrases
in prose-poetic manifesto letters
reaggaetón
drawn from mythlandscapes
& the liner notes of album presses
sampling or juggling different genres
moving maps, searching soles, or masked hidden faces
among the people policed into tight racial spaces.

Poetic Music Laundry List

Professor Shepp, Raw Poetic
You and I
A Love Supreme
The Nova Ghost Set   (AND)
Deconstructive Woodwind Chorus
The East Bay Dread Ensemble
The Mystic Horn Society
Molimo m'Atet
Sex Bob-Omb
Jossie and the Pussycats
Barry Jive & the Uptown Five
aka Sonic Death Monkey
aka Kathleen Turner Overdrive
Las Kellys The Kelly Affair The Carrie Nations
Fuck
The Archies
BUT
God Save
The Unrepentant Gays
Hedwig and The Angry Inch
Otis Day and the Knights
(Oh, how I loved them.
It was dark in the cinema that day,
and I kissed you)
Ellen Aim and The Attackers
CBGBsCB4
Eddie and The Cruisers
Figrin D'an and the Moodal Nodes
Stillwater
Citizen Dick
Slavoj & The Masterbators

Jazz Sabbath
(Here come)
The Lords of the Underworld

To leave your body before death arrives
and walk towards the Sun from the dark,
listen to & recite the previous incantation,
while gyrating on a turntable.

Charon

Dear friend across the river
come 'n take us away from here,
away from this hellish red,
dad
come back 'n
carry us away from here,
my sister and I
woke up from the war
to the sound and noise
of the silence that allows
the chatter of my voice
to become a shockwave in return
washing away the pain.

Turn around
put my ear down to the ground
and hear the stories being told
we've been searching to behold
the elements underground
with which stories will be told
       again
       at war's end
       when we'll be bold
enough
to ask for whom the bell has tolled.

My back now to the world
to the inquisitor's world
the night of the world
to the witch who was smiling when my mother died,
who

took my mirror and soul,
but they say
once you turn
they'll try to kill us
          break us   hate us
so we'll never be saints
brother sister
only enemies.

My beautiful
Ix-
you and I
are ready
to make our next move
dance better
even if they kill us
break us
hate us
for here we are
listening to the freakwaves
protopoppunks
and skaindls
sldniaks

gyrating on a turntable
getting' caught stealin'
a little blue ball,
the fire of sound,
chased by policeniaks
          who want to jail us into racial
                              spaces.

                    We won't let them,
we'll dance-fight

until you or I get our heads bashed up.
But don't worry.
I will move to the side,
and you shall get a pass.

I've seen your face here
under the tables
underground
you can tell me your fears and fantasies
what brings you
round
here
to the lost & found
down underground

down underground
we found,
you and I,
we found
the Hounds of the Underground.
Two children fleeing
the war-torn lands of our childhood
to end up fleeing
war-torn ExLondon.

Sit. Down.

down underground
with the hounds
in the undercity
we're growing up and gettin' out
lookin' to write our own stories,
even if the song remains the same,
the same ol' story

of topside and bottomdown
down
down underground.

We swore never to betray each other,
our people,
but fight for them,
o tell me,
don't you recall
when we painted on that wall
a giant middle finger,
and promised each other
to keep our little secrets.

One day this city will respect us,
'cause we found
in exLondon bedlam
the backrooms and back corridors
through which every boudoir in Clapham
became a light beam,
whisking us away,
as if by sorcerer's magick,
to other games
in other planets
not this one.

I woke up to the sounds.
They kill us break us hate us.
We were just girls back then
You and I
You're now my lover
sister
brother

and I
an enemy of the state
'cause I've dwelled in the arcane
mirror-souls
books
darkspells
and sounds

be-bebop
free jazz
drill and grime
punk and funk
with Archie, Raw Poetic & Damu the Fudgemunk

weird videogames
post-futurity child toys
but
as the blind prophet said
that post
might turn out
to have been
premature
 after all.

She Raves Tragedy

She raves a tragedy
      she might
      or might not like it
but once she takes to the stage
she contains
only half   of it
once she takes up the fight
she unleashes
the other half
herself all ears and eyeballs
exploding atoms, rays, and fire
leaping and lifting her
above
across the space
they just passed
she defeats the Moirai
just like fire would
but
the ground has no open mouth
but
it swallows any and all
Fates or fate
and the girl
she looks beautiful
in her spotted sun o' the night
jaguar ensemble
once she takes to the stage
and sets it on fire.

Jaguar and leopard
her tail in the leotard

she sure looks good
ascending from the cave to the stage
from Antigone to Sailor Moon
too chic to leap but ready to strike
she knows true tragedy
like love
is atmospheric
gravitational
it surrounds us
slices us
claws are laws
tear us apart

           revealing
what she hides
behind the silks and sequins of
Spain
Adrian
or Bob Mackie

She raves a simulation of tragedy
an imitation of life

           and as such
           she is true to life
           truer than most
since nothing is authentic
unmasked or not theatrical,
at least in the sense that there is no outside
to the totality of things,
when a Black woman speaks,
only internal perspectives
which are partial
and reflect one another
as the facets of one of her diamonds

no fate here
no vision of an ultimate judgment
or the perfect coincidence
between knowledge and being
yielding to calculation
an unknowable path

and there's the tragedy

                       her tragedy
                       our tragedy

like the cosmos repeating itself
after an unimaginable time
but there's no Angel of History
to notice it
no justice
just us

true tragedy
is atmospheric and
gravitational
(she)
goes back to the cave
to find in the dark
the elements of story
that
when put together
bring
memory
back
and behind it
time

(she)
shows us that to tell anything, to register it

she must take a small step to the side
make present her subtle difference
from it
so that being and knowledge never fully coincide

tale & tragedy are atmospheric and
gravitational
in that regard
they
can only happen
when she takes to the stage
when she takes up the fight
a black woman speaks
she sings
she stands
afloat, goes up, comes back to the light
she speaks
she sings
she stands
at the abarian point between field forces
burning in her path those who burn crosses
afloat
up
and light

like Greta Garbo
Tippi Hedren
David Bowie

or Judy Garland
telling the Great and Powerful

                                        (Oz)

he can fuck

O dear Judy.
Her death
in time
before time
on 22 June, 1969
was the spark
that ignited the night
of New York on 3 July
when firestarters of all kinds
set the city ablaze
a rave for the times

she did
like I did
just like fire would do
set alight
our council state flat
on 3 June, 2069
burning the inquisitors and the police
        for shutting down Bowie
        and Judy Garland
        whose death sparked a fire
        that burns
        from Stonewall to Popham State
        bringing Suella & The Liar
        to their final fate

She speaks
She is black, mayan,
'n slave
so we don't have to

las bolleras
las galas

las trans
las marías
las latinas en drag
Hu y Antígona
Sophia, Zoe y Nayra
You

a Black woman speaks
she sings
she stands

        she shows us no goddess
        will come down
        to save us

Rita Hayworth
Liz Taylor
Frida Kahlo
Ramona
Lady Gaga

They rave justice
Speak sing 'n dance
doing justice
raving vengeance
because justice
is never ours

She raves revenge
           on the lords of this dark land
while we plot on it
on sleepless
nights

their revolt
may be domesticated by the market
a failed revolution
a vicarious triumph

But it don't matter.

We don't need a goddess.
She doesn't need us either.

Call and Response

On the phone
after listening to her tape
the police officers asked her name

I gave them only the middle
finger

"Music"
a mask made of wind, of wrack
by which if
by wind it meant soul it meant
salvage[13]

not savage

a certain wariness of culture
masks
and identity masks
and performance

music
subjected to subjunctive relay work of qualm
verging on evacuating the light & sound
masquerade
(performance also, then, in that sense)
that music is, the graphic and acoustic masquerade

---

[13]Nathaniel Mackey, *Whatsaid Serif* (San Francisco: City Lights, 1998) 21.

that poetry is[14]

possessed or problematic speech
the thing found in the dark

call and

[14]Nathaniel Mackey, *Paracritical Hinge* (Iowa City: University of
Iowa Press, 2018) 233.

Call and _____ (2)

There is something in common

                    between

poetry
love
an atom
García Lorca's cante jondo
and Blck music
        a
a rapidly vibrating guitar string
making waves
lifting her up
out of the cave

And as it happens

                    with

poetry
love
an atom
García Lorca's cante jondo
and Blck music
        a
when she speaks
she sings
she   takes up the fight
        takes to the stage
in the waves
you can never see the _____ itself.

Centrifugal Poem

It begins with an ironic wave to the lord of the court
it bids all givens goodbye
it bides time for what words will not do
                    what perspective will not do
                    what the novel will not do
                    what the joy of work
        and the consolations of philosophy will not do

The joy of work and the consolations of philosophy
accrue their primitive accumulation value
to a horizon it wants to get across and beyond,
abandoning the joy of work, the mastery of the novel,
and the consolations of philosophy,
or seeking new ones.

It will, of course, be marginalised
especially when listened to
on the phone on tape or on a digital file
sent from the   island   of Papayal
by the wordsmith of Las Pavas
or spoken by a Blck girl coming back
from the bowels of the earth

Blck centrifugal writing and indigenous alternate voices
have been
continue to be
multiply marginalised
sent back to relic time
unremittingly
but why would it be otherwise?

At a time when...
critical discourse battens on identity obsession
centrifugal writing reorients identity
in ways that defy prevailing divisions of labour.
In the face of widespread fetishisation of collectivity,
it dislocates collectivity,
flies from collectivity,
wants to make flight a condition of collectivity.[15]

It lets go of the Angel of History in favour of the Ghost of
Chance.
This is one of the lessons it
(critique)
 has learned from Blck music.

It is, like any other art, not new but imaginative,
 inventive,
productive
and/our outside.

To the extent that it addresses the wings of
and dresses in the wings of
all resistances
indigenous to its practice and medium,
ranging from the amorous touch of love
to the agonistic embrace of deep sound
the fission of an atom
the rapid vibration of a string or a drum skin

sending its fire
in all directions

---

[15] Nathaniel Mackey, "Destination Out" in *Paracritical Hinge*, 239
for quote and the source of this poem.

in waves
but in them you cannot see the _____s.

Demonic rub,
it speaks in alternate voices,
recorded
on a tape
a digital file
on the phone
time
and again.

Something unknown
doing
we don't know what
which is the total sum
of the joys of our work
and the consolations of our philosophy.

Do not wear them,
Wings,
as if they were the stuff
and essence of our community
but only eight slithy toves gimbaling and gyrating
on a turntable
in the oxygen wave,
particle and wave,
the
remains of the subtle fire wave that made
Ix the jinn and Hu girl
together like lovers in a whirlwind

in demonic embrace.

The centrifugal poet is not nearly so concerned
with describing the facts
as with creating light & sound
image-systems
that make something happen in us
which lift us up
and bring us dancing back down
to the brief history of this instant.

Lords Doubt

After listening on the phone on the tape

her voice
digitally altered
on a Teenage Engineering PO
sounding like the centrifugal destination
of a post-expectant futurity

the Lords of Xibalbá
asked the blind prophet
and his deaf companion

Why haven't we vanquished the twin lovers?

That was their moment of fall and ruin.
But
wait
there's a history to every instant
no matter how brief
and this one is no exception.

Hu and Ix
had already spoken
to Xulú, the blind prophet
and Pacam, his deaf companion.

We've felt a promise, premise, and premonition,
they told them.

That the lords of this dark country
will use firestones and mirrors

to break us kill us hate us
that they're in doubt
thinking what to do
that they're measuring
with precision
the size of this instant
how to seize it,
grab hold of it.

They will ask you how
to break us kill us hate us.

They will say:
break their bones with a chainsaw
put them in a conveyor-belt
throw them in the crusher
make them dust.
Put them in a field and bomb the bastards!

It isn't convenient, you will say to them,
for they will be reborn after the first day

Then they will say:
hang them from the cannibal trees
splinter the names
use them as white paint
to cover the who gave the order graffiti with low-lying spray,
make them invisible, get them lost.

It isn't convenient, you will say to them,
for they will be reborn after the second day.

Then they will say:

take them on a carpet-bombing helicopter ride
push them from up high
make them fall.

It isn't convenient, you will say to them,
for they will be reborn after three days.

Then, exasperated, they will say:
What would you have us do?

And you will say to them:
the lovers,
they're poets aren't they?
They're searching for the elements of story.
Isn't that why they came down underground?
If so,
make them perform.
Performance is a most bothersome and inconvenient word
for writerly poets
like being thrown into a river after being burnt in an oven fire.

Sight-specific prose poem, or not

Performance is a bothersome and inconvenient word for
writerly poets, someone said. I agree. Spoken word, poetry
slams, lit festivals, and word jams have made the term and
what we do tantamount to or even synonymous with the antics
of theatricality and spectacle: a recourse to monumentality,
to the plight of the hero placed in a hinging moment of
catastrophe, the declamatory, persuasive or pleasing rhetoric,
and the inner motifs of a scandal. Such tactics have become
widespread in the framing of news narratives, in so-called
autofiction, and in the novel. They aim at propping up words
and sounds or helping them appear more effective, suggestive,
or persuasive. It makes sense in times like these, now that
every single one of our aspects and innermost intentions can be
captured on screen by a smartphone device or a camera. They
work pushing forces like the obsidian mirrors of old. And as
in the Rage Against the Machine song, those who work to
push forces are often the same that burn crosses. Underpinning
such attitudes is the assumption that words are inert when
left on their own or at least weaker than marble architectures
and unchangeable frames. Vegetable-like. The history of
that assumption would take us back to colonial times in the
Americas. When European chroniclers marvelled at the oratory
powers of indigenous wordsmiths, at the same time as they
would dismiss such popular practices of fine performance art
as relics that attested to the myrtle-like nature of their soul and
mind. Which these chroniclers supposed as fluid as the rain
and rivers of the forests, and as changing, multitudinous, and
excessive in their appetite as the vegetation or the predators
of the jungle. And, therefore, weaker in comparison to the
strength of the fortress architectures and fortitude virtues of

Christian mores. It may not be a coincidence that the tropes expressing these assumptions, coming from the visualisations of martial architecture, Euclidean geometry, and defensive mentalities became established around the seventeenth century. At the same time as notions of spatial theatre and gothic symbolism engendered and pervaded a culture of political spectacle, expansion, and takeover of space from European centres to the rest of the world. Beginning but not only in the Americas. The tropes, presuppositions, and the basic assumptions informing such attitudes can be seen in the frontispiece of the book *Leviathan*, itself a symbol and trope for the beast of darkness and order-out-of-chaos, published in 1651. That kind of illusionistic representation or theatre must be contrasted with presence and opposed to the perhaps older political potential of presentational image-systems in which landscape, light & sound come together to make present other spaces and time dimensions. In these imaginary domains the past, being past, is brought to bear on the present and the future in a way that can make present, for us, the many variations and possibilities that lie ahead of us. Not because we can know them as a certain path into the future but precisely because we can't. They show us that the future is open. The contrast between presence and theatricality means we can no longer describe in an evaluative way the so-called primitive mind *as if* it lacked the capacity to conceive of a distinction between truth and falsehood, or *as if* it lacked the strength of will to sustain that distinction. We cannot speak of such things *as if* there were a hinging moment when the mind finally develops its powers of abstraction and critical reason becomes ironic. Such "as if" discrimination between "our" newly formed (modern) subjectivity and "their" presumed lack of it is pedantic. And most likely unwarranted, as a growing mountain of archaeological evidence shows. It would be better to see in that contrast the presence in language of varying experiences of spatiality and time. Including theatricality. Without making one experience exhaustive of reality or normatively prior over others. It's the experience of space which emerges from the baroque period onwards, the theatrical screen, the mirror of the soul and its devices, that allow us to express the world and its relation to others in it in terms that invite comparison with older image-systems and devices that permit a participatory experience. For example, dark glasses and obsidian mirrors can be brought together with the black mirrors of our smartphone screens as creative of the inscrutable and inaccessible image that invites a great deal of participation and completion, as in call-and-response formats common to black music, writerly poetry and videogames. These are distillations of a general dialectic of concealment and revelation that isn't culturally or identity-specific but specific to the site of the encounter between Christian Europeans and Amerindians less prone to believing in belief from the baroque period onwards. Such dialectic is also the creative space of the public, with political implications. Think of that space as the abarian point between two field forces, or even more. A point which is crucial to plot one's motion between worlds such as the Earth and the Moon or the skies above and the underground. In modern times this means to take seriously the question that comes to us from the literatures of supposedly pre-theatrical times: can we move backwards or downwards looking forwards? Or the same: is there such a thing as an open future, for example a future without mirror-souls or screens? The screen isn't just a technological innovation or a man-made clever device, but the object we can use to think about the experience of the animated word as a key ingredient in a specific organisation of time and space. And by extension, of memory. Specific encounters in which part of the fiction is that there is no fiction, that there is no screen there. This in no way means that presence is a thing of the "primitive" past.

It persists in the shape of a cave, the underground and the experience of the underground we have had while following Hu girl and Ix through their katabasis. An experience that is basic to the telling of stories, to the extent that it may be the elemental medium of poetry and story itself. Only that the moments of ecstasy, immediacy, impacting action or the abarian moments are couched in, happen in, and become present to us from within the confines of the cave and the underground. Which is to say that our very desire for the cave is theatrical, as inherent to the life of the word as it is of our drive to and away from death. Persistence of theatre, then. And persistence of presence. "And," not "or." There's no need to up our words with performativity because the latter is internal to our language, an effect of theatre and of presence peering to us through the fourth wall, not outside of it. There's no outside of the fourth wall. And that is why we can look at the lens of the camera. The take won't be rubbish.

Sound-specific prose poem, or not

Words tend to be regarded nowadays as needing help,
embellishment, photoshop, and make up. And are, therefore,
presumed ugly, decrepit or even death if left on their own.
They are condemned and damned. Poor words uttered by
poorer people, the stupid masses that simply are. Better, then,
to leave important matters to important people. The masters
of the universe, who can perform better. Our current lords
and heroes (yes, we can be heroes too, but as Bowie said,
just for one day). Me, I can't perform. This I said when I
was asked to perform as part of the Spoken Word Festival
in Southbank. I know, perhaps it was one of those hinging
moments when destiny catches up. Life or Death. I know, I
was arrogant, paraphrasing Nathaniel Mackey and Wilson
Harris that way, rolling them into one without proper credits.
But what can I say? I'm just a bookish poet, a writerly one.
And writerly poets are bothered by the word performance.
Writerly poets are advocates of the animated word; devotees
of what shamans call the inner life of the word. Meaning it
can create imaginary domains and theatrical spaces. These
can be mapped. One such mapping shows that there is an
extensive "sound geography" along the Northwest Amazon
border of Brazil, Venezuela, and Colombia that consists
of crucial locations, borders and thresholds, of creolised
Arawakan, Akan, and other invention traditions. This includes
waterfalls with petroglyphs and stone formations in which the
wind composes whispers and whistles that suggest to the ear
(patient enough to learn how to listen) the beginning of the
universe at the Hipana rapids, the first death, and its rebirth
through the underground quest and rebirth of the twins (like
Hu and Ix). This sound geography and the elements of story
found in it simply point to a broader sense of reciprocity and

responsibility for the structures that hold together a material world – which we seehear as patterns that not only exist but must be continuously animated & preserved. It is said that those who came before us left traces of their presence at these sites, as fragments or ruins of memories, and it is up to us to re-make them. These sites are thresholds or portals. They are positioned not only in space but also in time. Let us use the term *mythscape* to refer to the large landscape in which such thresholds can be found. A comparable notion may be the "Dreamtime" of the Aborigenes of Australia. My journey as Hu made it possible to plot a mythscape map. It contains:

(1) Hipana, as the birthplace of the universe, of humanity, and of Kuwai, also known as Ix -a living being figured as a set of flutes & trumpets engaged in a sort of jazz improv.

(2) A rapids slightly downriver from Hipana, which is the emergence site of the group my abuela came from, located in the upper Guainia River around the town of Maroa. It is the responsibility of the palabrero wordsmiths who reside there to guard the rapids from destruction or defilement such as can be brought by miners and settlers who often pawn their lives to the Lords of Death and the paramilitary led by Señor Matanza. They ensure that everyone who visits can see, hear, and learn from the sound beats of the boulders and petroglyphs, one of which shows the "false Kuwai", the Lords of Death, and the trials they put the twins through: the "pain of the whip", a "sieve for filtering manioc" or a mirror-soul, and spirals making present "sounds of flutes" coming from under the ground.

(3) Nearby, in Uaracapory, on the upper Vaupés, is the site of the Great Tree of Sustenance, which existed at the time of the First Universe. When the Great Tree was cut down, humanity obtained food for their gardens and the wordsmiths, pajés, and shamans gained their storytelling

powers. Look for them in the poetry of Alejandro
Jodorowsky and René Ménil or Suzanne Césaire. Sorry,
I'm at it again. An arrogant fool dropping names, again.

The thing is, when you asked me to perform poetry for
ladies and lords, I found that word most inconvenient
and bothersome. What did you expect? My abuela was a
Colombian living in the UK. After the fall, I grew up in a
doomeddomed Council Estate in ExLondon. She would tell
me the stories of Maroa and Uaracapory, of the Great Tree
of Sustenance and the place they called The Garden. She
spoke of guerrillas turning into bulls to get the conservative
militias at night. She told me about my father's library. So,
I turned up a pedantic arsehole, reading fantasy tales to my
sisters and my friends. After the Church Council banned
them, I would hide a few inside the dolls abuela helped me
put together, sawn from discarded parts in the manner of
monsters. She taught me how to deal with mythic matter,
dark matter, and other deviant substances. She was shaman,
or wordsmith. She pretended to be, if you prefer, so she
could make a buck or two selling liquids, psychedelics, and
shit. I learned from her. I learned hard and I learned it fast.
She said I was her enforcer, retribution, and vengeance.
Lady Justice. Small wonder, they sent their moral police,
their inquisitors and witches after me. I was just a girl. I
had no other choice than running and returning. And run
and turn and return is all I have done. I convinced some
smuggler friends to get my sis and I out of town in one of
those DIY sub-boats dealers use to cross the channel into
war-torn Europe. During the crossing, a witch got to us.
They hate us. They wanted to kill us, break us. They took
everyone and left me for dead. No mirror, no ID, no name.
They took my sis too. I must have spent weeks stranded
at sea. Until I made it here. Wherever here is. Other side

of the ocean, between the Caribbean and the Anaconda River. Carried by the Gulf Stream, I guess, even though they say it collapsed many years ago. The AMOC global conveyor belt. Turns out climate meltdown was non-linear. We didn't know what degrees of warming will cause what aspects of the Earth-system to go bunkers. It did. Half the world drowned. The other half were cooked alive. So, here I was, at the entrance of a tall edifice part of which was immersed between the Caribbean Sea and the Orinoco River. It looked like a cave. The men guarding the entrance had damaged skin, scorpion-red. One of them comes to us, *to eat as if flesh of the gods*, they said. *Two thirds goddess, the rest badass*, I replied. Why have you come on such a long journey? I'm looking for a place called The Garden. I'm on a salvage operation to rescue the elements of story. Ah, you're looking for Utnapishtim. He built himself a boat and was spared by the deluge. People around here think the gods gave him life everlasting. He has plenty of stories to tell. He's on the last floor of this edifice. But there are many floors in this building, many leagues to walk from undercity to topside, and it's all dark. No light in there, and the heat is oppressive, people fall under with solitude and sadness. A desolate place. I entered. I did. When I had travelled one league the darkness became so thick, I could see nothing behind me and nothing ahead of me. Fever struck me after six leagues, and there was like a fog in my mind. My memory is not good because of that. Not factual, unreliable, so I didn't know how to go back and recalled only fragments. Vague images of my dead mother, my escape, a lost sis or a lover. It's all like a spectre haunting. At the end of twelve floors or leagues a boy found me. He shined in my eyes as if the sun itself were streaming in or a star ascended a stare when I shut my eyelids. He claimed to have been a girl once and was

162

about the same age as my lost sister. Perhaps I rolled them into one. He became my brothersister, my lover. We got each other, stood by each other while transiting this dark, awful place. Then, you came. You claimed to be the lord of this land. You came to us saying we were robbers. We were hungry, so we stole your food. We were thirsty, so we took your water. We smelled bad, so we took your flowers, made perfumes, and bathed in them. We cleansed ourselves. You came to us saying we were robbers, pirates. But we have taken these things as gifts nature offers and presented gifts to the mother to express our thanks. The way abuela had taught me. How could we know you claimed property over them? And what if you did? After all, all things are common luxury. Your republic and borders look small when compared to our universal republic. Not to mention the extent of the disaster in here or out there. All things are common luxury. Fruits grew on trees, first. Maize seeds grow in the fields, which abuela taught me how to grind to make cornbread. The water, and the flowers floating in it. You put us on trial. To break us and kill us because you hate us. Because I'm blck. We played your game. The black woman sang. We renamed ourselves. I was Hu. My sis was Ix. You outed us through videodrome, cut us in the house of knives, froze us in the house of cold ice and scolded our feet in fire. In the house of the jaguars, a vampire-like repo man took my head as payment for our debts. Music and the birds who sing bass brought me back when I thought I had lost my mind. Now here I am. You and the other lords said *perform, embrace the deadness of the word as your inner wound*. Because I'm a girl you say I have an inner wound. But I'm writerly dancer and poet too. For me there's no performance. It is not me performing, it's the words on the page and the sounds in the air that do. And it is the words and the sounds that will defeat you.

163

Light My Fire

Embracing each other
Hu and Ix bowed their heads to the earth
and exploded precipitating a fire.
They died together.

The Lords of Xibalbá
called Xulú and Pacam at once.
We did it
We hated them so we broke them and killed them.
What must we do with their bones?
The blind prophet and his deaf companion performed the
rites of divination and
told the lords to grind them and throw them into the river.

But the mother bones did not go very far.
Flowing all the way to the bottom they transformed into
bright young girls.
Their faces glowing like the sun and the moon themselves.

Do not ask how long is an instant
or a second
Do not ask to measure with forensic precision its succession
or to calculate its length and duration
for the moment you ask that
is the moment of your fall and ruin
you will mistake a perfect solid for reality
the inquisition's fantasies for fantasies
and miss all that flows, transit, and transforms.

Here they come.
In flow,
Transit,
and transformed.
The twins
Hu and Ix
Reborn.
On their backs,
They bring sunlight.
Time.
And stories.
As old as time.

Epilogue

Post-expectant Futurity.

We stand on lost
loose
oddly elevated ground, the
apotheosis of war
in the lands of our childhood.

This is no glib-materialisation
of loss or fabricated sound, the
anti-expectant gist of which is
what the prophet warned us about.

That 'post' might turn out
to be 'premature'.

Not be what it wanted to be
not post but oddly elevated underground, the
ingenious outdoing of disingenuously harboured hopes
of post-expectant futurity.

Noise or atomistic l/edge
of post-expectant futures running aground, the
multiply-possessed before body before we hit
the ground running into full mediation without reference to
the original body
a single note or primary self.

Even though its multiply-pinned message
gave an operatic lift to the post-expectant ground, the
quantum-qualitative nonsense sound of cyberpunk prophets

dreaming of the network gridling the globe as a nascent life-
form or absolute spirit

but it is lost loose ground, another let there be light ground
and goad rolled into one

Part seismic spirit, part alternate voice
like Movement 4 of Floating Points moving around, the
auto-inscriptive lilt a theatre to not coin a phrase
inasmuch as what we want is real.

What this meant was that want
walked with real across fantastic grounds, the
ripped-ruptural affirmation of post-expectant promises,
premises, and premonitions
running thru it all rolled into one.

The odd post-expectant way it had
of rolling promise, premise, and premonition round into
one, the
whole piece into one piece
into one mixed-metaphorical sound not ground.

Here we stand if stand could be said
what we did when we went underground, the
clubs in which we played on decks mixed-metaphorical sounds

conveyor-belt
carpet-ride
mist-pointillist plank
splint low-lying spray

of post-expectant futurity

and dance

not tragedy.

Political Poetry of the Future

This is a rhythmic overlay
between
Qhipnayra uñtasis sarnaqapxañani
and
the meticulous realisation of our dream's desire.

I

A bass-soaked overlay
reverb saturates,
the line of succession
and
temporal orientation
towards an apocalyptic end.
It opens an interval in timespace.

II

The lowest rhythmic interval
becoming music or wave.
An axion mass scale wave.
It acts
sometimes
as if made of billiard-ball parts
and other times
sloshing like watery waves.
Waves coming together in rhythmic overlay
to create a super wave
that no archive can place
in a final resting place.

III

The revolution will not be televised, he said.
But our protest will be sampled.
A bass-soaked overlay
That reverb saturates
Black matter
opening
La frontera border en el fin.
A void vortex,
an open wound.

IV

Heridas abiertas
con
Venas abiertas
And void vórtices
Vorágine verde y hojarasca
A leaf storm's shocking return, in
whirlpools of water
from where everything comes
to which everything returns
for there's no loss
No beginning
No end
But
base suspense,
bass-soaked relay
outside of today's visual array.

V

Consider the power of words in the age of self-image:

'US-headquartered companies bought the
rights
to water in other countries.'
South of the border.
'These companies are
strangers to the gods of those waters, were
not
formed from them, have never said Gracias
to
those waters, never prayed to those waters
have never been cleansed by those waters.'[16]
Is there any chance the gods may come back angry?

VI

That is why we protest.
Not the human we
are not.
But
The thirst protests.
The hunger protests.
The lack of air protests.
That is why we protest.
We know
The revolution will not be televised,
But the protest will be sampled.
Cut-up, cut-in, and overlayed, intervals between imaginals
Or
Rhythmic sound overlays
to
seehear

---

[16] Natalie Diaz, Postcolonial Love Poem (London: Faber & Faber, 2020) 70.

and
sensethink
Not to contemplate
But to dance
& axion.

VII

Therefore
no wonder
and
no fear
but word cinemas,
dwelling,
rambling
wandering
We trans move
Looking forwards
Moving backwards
Backwards
 we dancewalk
Searching in futures past for light
of what is to come
but not yet.
We walk
Together
In alliance
without allegiance
Rhythm wise
but not straight
In bass-soaked intervals
Until we reach the crossroads
where the old has died but hangs on zombie-like
and the new wants to be born

But not yet.

VIII

Here the future begins,
back to the heart
back to the womb
back to the matter
of futures past
which never stop
if we stop
thinking metamerically,
we may distinguish
diametrically
 vertiginously
The light of lighthouses
From the lanterns of wreckers
wishing to lure us aground
to loot us
and slave us.

IX

We may not want to know it
But we can't shake it off
The feeling
that
We must break free from these chains.
Shed this body.
For it is not so much that the body is a kind of clothing,
But clothing which is a kind of body.
It as the poet says:
'Take my body and make of it—

A Nation.'[17]
But one without confession
Or allegiance.
For it assumes the homogenous body of a Nation.
'An American way of forgetting Natives.
Discover them with City. Crumble them by
City.
Erase them into Cities named for their
Bones, until
You are the new Natives of your new Cities ...
[But] Who lies beneath [these] streets, [these] universities,
[these] art
Museums?'[18]
She asks.

X

Let's cross the border in the opposite direction.
Go south
at sea
to see
really see
dance
& seehear
A rhythmic overlay
A bass-soaked relay
That reverb saturates without delay
For we can no longer wait.

---

[17] Natalie Diaz, Postcolonial Love Poem, 56.

[18] Natalie Diaz, Postcolonial Love Poem, 64.